my first
COOKIE & CAKE
DECORATING
BOOK

my first
COOKIE & CAKE
DECORATING
BOOK

35 techniques and recipes
for children aged 7-plus

CICO **Kidz**

Published in 2017 by CICO Kidz

An imprint of Ryland, Peters & Small Ltd

20–21 Jockey's Fields   341 E 116th St

London WC1R 4BW   New York, NY 10029

www.rylandpeters.com

10 9 8 7 6 5 4 3 2 1

A CIP catalog record for this book is available from the
Library of Congress and the British Library.

ISBN: 978-1-78249-492-8

Printed in China

Series consultant: Susan Akass
Editor: Clare Sayer
Designer: Alison Fenton
Step artworks: Rachel Boulton
Animal artworks: Hannah George
Templates: Rachel Boulton
For recipe and photography credits, see page 128

Editor: Dawn Bates
Art director: Sally Powell
Production controller: David Hearn
Publishing manager: Penny Craig
Publisher: Cindy Richards

Safety guidelines

• This book contains recipes made with raw
eggs. It is prudent for more vulnerable people,
such as pregnant and nursing mothers, babies
and very young children, invalids and the elderly,
to avoid uncooked dishes made with eggs.
• Some of the recipes contain nuts and should
not consumed by anyone with a nut allergy.
• Always ask for adult help when using sharp
knives and when using a stovetop or a hot oven.

Measurement guidelines

• All spoon measurements are level unless
otherwise specified.
• Both US cup sizes or imperial and metric
measurements have been given. Use one set of
measurements only and not a mixture of both.
• Ovens should be preheated to the specified
temperatures. All ovens work slightly differently.
We recommend using an oven thermometer
and suggest you consult the maker's handbook
for any special instructions, particularly if you
are cooking in a fan-assisted oven, as you will
need to adjust temperatures according to the
manufacturer's instructions.

Contents

Introduction

When you learn to cook, baking is often one of the first things you try because it's so much fun to see the mixture transform into tasty cakes and cookies. It is even more fun if you can go on to decorate them and create something that looks amazing too.

You may have a celebration coming up—a birthday, a Christmas party, Mother's Day—and want to create something special for the day; or you may just want to enjoy learning new techniques. Whatever your reason for wanting to decorate a cake or some cookies, *My First Cookie and Cake Decorating Book* will get you started.

Opposite, you will find a list of useful kitchen equipment as well as some important tips and techniques on how to bake safely and successfully.

In Chapter One, you'll find the basic recipes to create most of the cakes and cookies (a few projects use different recipes and these are given within the project). Chapter Two introduces you to lots of different decorating techniques, from shaping cakes to covering them with fondant icing, to making chocolate decorations and "flooding" cookies for a perfect smooth surface. Everything you need to get started is here. In Chapter Three there are fun step-by-step cookie projects and Chapter Four is full of creative cake projects. Get going with these to practice all your new skills.

To help you make a success of your decorating, we have graded the projects with one, two, or three smiley faces—see opposite. Level 1 projects are the ones to begin with, as these are the easiest. Level 2 projects are a little trickier and are good for practicing skills. Level 3 are the most challenging—they may need you to make and frost quite big cakes or use more complicated decorating techniques, but they will produce some spectacular cakes and cookies.

And remember, these projects are only the beginning. Once you have mastered the decorating techniques, you can let your imagination go wild to create your own extraordinary cakes and cookies!

Kitchen safety—read this before you start cooking!

• Always wash your hands before you start making your cakes and cookies.

• Tie long hair back so that it is out of the way.

• Wear an apron to keep your clothes clean.

• Make sure your ingredients are fresh and within their use-by date.

• Use oven mitts when holding hot pans or dishes and whenever you put your cookies or cakes into the oven or take them out.

• Use a chopping board when using a sharp knife or metal cookie cutters—this protects the work surface and will help to stop the knife from slipping.

• Keep your work surface clean and wipe up any spills on the floor so that you don't slip.

• Don't forget to clear up afterward!

Safety Tip

When using sharp knives, electrical equipment, the stovetop (hob), microwave, or oven, always ask an adult to help you.

Kitchen equipment

Strainer (sieve)	Mixing bowls in different sizes	Wire whisk
Sharp knives	Heatproof glass bowls	Rubber spatula
Scissors	Microwave-safe bowls	Rolling pin
Palette knife	Saucepans	Cake pans
Cutting board	Wooden spoon	Muffin pans
Egg cup	Measuring pitcher (jug)	Baking sheets
Plastic wrap (clingfilm)	Weighing scales and measuring cups	Wire cooling rack
Baking parchment	Measuring spoons	Cookie cutters
Paper towel (kitchen paper)		

Project levels

Level 1
These have only a few stages or require just a little adult help.

Level 2
These include more stages, some difficult techniques, and may require some adult help.

Level 3
These are more challenging and have more steps.

Tips and techniques

When baking, it's important to be precise. By measuring all your ingredients accurately, preheating your oven to the correct temperature, and preparing your cake pans and trays in advance, you're more likely to create successful bakes.

Using an oven

• The first thing you need to do for most of the baking recipes is to turn on the oven so that it preheats. This is because the oven needs to be hot enough to bake your cookies and cakes and it takes a little while to heat up.

• The recipe instructions always tell you at what temperature to set your oven. Ask an adult to show you how to set the temperature correctly.

• On most ovens there is a light, which goes out when the oven reaches the temperature you have set, and then it is ready to use.

• It is recommended to use the middle shelf of the oven for most baking needs. Make sure that there is space above it for your cakes to rise.

• Always use oven mitts when putting food into the oven or taking it out and put hot baking sheets or cake pans on a heatproof board or trivet so that you don't burn the work surface.

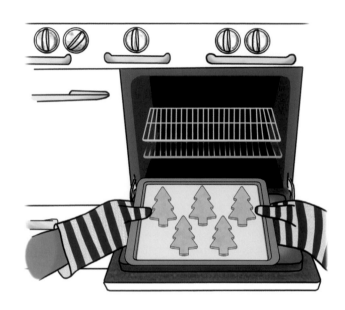

Preparing your pans

When you make a cake or cookies, after you have switched on the oven, you must next prepare your pan. This stops the cake mixture from sticking as it cooks so it will be easy to turn out. Grease the pan by rubbing all over the inside with a little oil or butter on a paper towel. Most cake recipes also tell you to base-line a pan with baking parchment—to do this draw around the pan on baking parchment, cut out the shape, and pop it into the base.

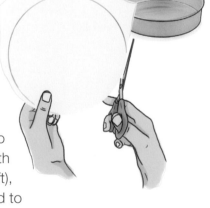

When baking cookies on a baking sheet, your recipe will tell you whether you need to grease the sheet with a little butter (see left), or whether you need to line the sheet with a piece of baking parchment that you have cut to the right size.

Using the stovetop (hob)

- Always ask an adult before using the stovetop.
- When using the stovetop, make sure that saucepan handles don't stick out over the front of the stovetop where you could knock them off.
- Don't have the heat too high—it is easy to burn your food.
- Always remember to turn off the heat when you've finished cooking.
- When you take a pan off the stovetop, always put it onto a heatproof board or trivet so that you don't burn the work surface.

Safety Tip

When using a microwave, always use microwave-safe bowls and never put anything metallic into the microwave.

Using knives

Good cooks must learn how to use knives properly and you should ask an adult to teach you. If you use it properly, a sharp knife is safer than a blunt one, because it won't slip, but you must hold the food firmly. Keep your fingers out of the way and always use a chopping board. Take care when washing up sharp knives too and always put them away carefully after use.

Weighing and measuring

Baking is a little like a science experiment and you need to have exact measurements in order for it to work successfully! This means weighing and measuring out the ingredients very carefully. This book uses two different types of measurements. Always follow one type and don't swap between the two in your recipe. Use either measuring cups or weighing scales for large quantities, and measuring spoons for smaller amounts. Check that the ingredients are level with the top of the spoon, unless the instructions tell you otherwise. Use measuring cups or pitchers (jugs) for liquids.

Butter

Almost all the recipes in this book use butter. For cakes and cookies unsalted butter is usually best. For cake recipes that need you to cream the butter with the sugar, the butter should be nice and soft, so take it out of the refrigerator in good time. For some cookie recipes you need to rub the butter into flour, so the butter should be chilled and hard.

Creaming butter and sugar

• Many cake recipes start with creaming butter and sugar, which means beating them together until they are well mixed and become pale and fluffy. This is an important stage because it makes the cakes light in texture.
• Always remember to take the butter out of the refrigerator at least half an hour before you need it, so it is soft and easy to cream.

• You can cream by hand with a wooden spoon but creaming is much quicker with electric beaters—always ask an adult to help with these.

Rubbing in

Some recipes ask you to rub butter into flour. To do this, first cut up chilled butter into small pieces and add it to the flour, Then, using your fingers, pick up small amounts of butter and flour and rub them together between your thumb and fingertips.

Keep picking up more of the mixture and rubbing it together. In this way, the butter gradually gets mixed into the flour until there are no lumps left and it looks like breadcrumbs.

Chilling and rolling dough

• Once you have made your cookie dough, most recipes will tell you to chill it in the refrigerator for a couple of hours. This keeps the butter in the dough solid and means that the cookies won't spread while they are baking in the oven. Simply flatten your ball of dough slightly and put into a resealable food bag or wrap tightly in plastic wrap (clingfilm).
• When you are ready to roll, make sure your work surface is clean and sprinkle with a little flour. Put some on your rolling pin too.
• When you roll, push the rolling pin down and away from you and try to get it an even thickness all over.
• Check that the dough isn't sticking to the surface by lifting and moving it between rolls. If it sticks, sprinkle more flour underneath it.

• Try not to handle the dough too much—it needs to stay cold and your hands will make it hot!
• When stamping out shapes with your cutters, press the cutter into the dough with your hands applying even pressure to get nice, neat cookies. Start right at the edge of the dough and cut the next cookie as close as possible to the previous shape so you can fit lots in before you need to gather up the trimmings and roll again.

Safety Tip

When heating in the microwave, stir the ingredient thoroughly. Even if it seems lukewarm on the outside, it could be burning hot inside. Stirring spreads the heat evenly and prevents hot spots.

Melting chocolate

Melting chocolate isn't difficult, but it does require a little patience. Melting it slowly is best because chocolate can easily overheat or scorch, leaving you with greasy, grainy lumps instead of yummy, smooth chocolate.

The best way is to use what is known as a "bain marie." Put the chopped chocolate into a heatproof bowl and ask an adult to help you set the bowl over a pan of barely simmering water, making sure that the bottom of the bowl doesn't touch the water. Stir until melted and smooth, then set aside to cool slightly.

You can also use a microwave—put the chocolate into a microwave-safe bowl and heat on low for 30 seconds. Stir, then heat again for another 30 seconds. Keep checking and stirring and when the chocolate is nearly melted, remove the bowl from the microwave and stir until smooth. If you stir with a plastic spoon you can leave it in the bowl when you microwave. If you use a metal spoon you must take it out each time.

chapter

Basic Recipes

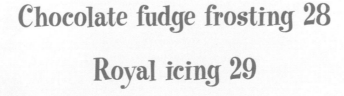

Vanilla cookies

Most of the cookie recipes in this book can be made with this basic vanilla recipe or the gingerbread cookie recipe on page 17. Remember to chill the dough for 2 hours or longer before rolling it out and shaping it into cookies. You'll also need to make sure your baked cookies are completely cold before decorating, otherwise the frosting will melt or slide off.

You will need

....

3½ cups (450 g) all-purpose (plain) flour, plus extra for dusting

pinch of salt

1¾ sticks (225 g) unsalted butter, at room temperature

1 cup (225 g) unrefined superfine (golden caster) sugar

1 large (UK medium) egg

½ teaspoon pure vanilla extract

2 baking sheets

non-stick baking parchment

makes 12–24

Tip

These cookies will keep unfrosted for 3 days in an airtight box. If they've been frosted, they should be eaten within 24 hours.

1 Place a large strainer (sieve) over a mixing bowl. Tip the flour and salt into the strainer and then sift them into the mixing bowl. Put the bowl to one side.

2 Put the soft butter and sugar into a large mixing bowl and beat them together with a wooden spoon until the mixture is soft, creamy, and pale. (If an adult is helping, you could use an electric beater.)

3 Break the egg into a small bowl and remove any pieces of shell. Beat the egg with a fork until the yolk has broken up and the mixture is a bit frothy. Add the beaten egg and vanilla extract to the creamed butter mixture and mix together well.

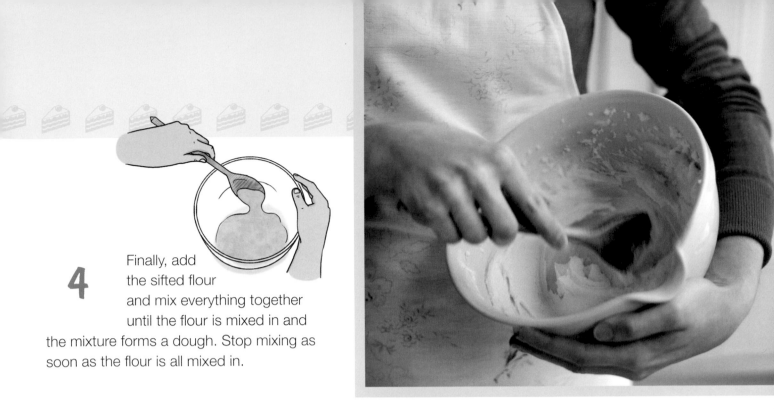

4 Finally, add the sifted flour and mix everything together until the flour is mixed in and the mixture forms a dough. Stop mixing as soon as the flour is all mixed in.

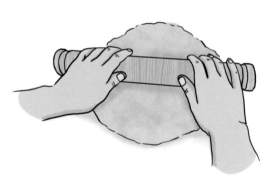

5 Tip the ball of dough out onto the work surface and flatten into a disc. Put the dough into a sealable food bag, or wrap it in plastic wrap (clingfilm), and chill in the refrigerator for 1–2 hours. Meanwhile, line two baking sheets with baking parchment.

6 You are now ready to roll out the dough and follow your recipe. Sprinkle a little flour on a clean work surface. Using a rolling pin, roll out the dough to a thickness of about ⅛ in. (3–4 mm). Stamp out shapes with cookie cutters and arrange on the prepared baking sheets. Gather up any scraps of cookie dough, knead very lightly to bring together into a ball, and roll out again to stamp out more cookies. Chill in the refrigerator for a further 15 minutes.

7 Ask an adult to turn the oven on to 350°F (180°C) Gas 4 and, when the oven is preheated, ask an adult to help you put the baking sheets on the middle shelf of the oven. Bake for 10–12 minutes until pale golden. Remove from the oven and leave the cookies to cool on the baking sheets before transferring to a wire rack to cool completely.

Gingerbread cookies

These cookies will keep unfrosted for 3 days in an airtight box. If they've been frosted, they should be eaten within 24 hours.

1 Ask an adult to turn the oven on to 350°F (180°C) Gas 4. Then carefully break the egg onto a plate and use an egg cup to separate the yolk from the white. You do not need the white for this recipe.

2 Put the light corn (golden) syrup and egg yolk in a small bowl and beat them together with a wooden spoon.

You will need

1 large (UK medium) egg

2 generous tablespoons light corn (golden) syrup

2 cups (200 g) all-purpose (plain) flour

¼ teaspoon baking powder

1½ teaspoons ground ginger

1 teaspoon ground cinnamon

¼ teaspoon ground nutmeg

pinch of salt

7 tablespoons (100 g) unsalted butter, chilled and diced

⅓ cup (75 g) light muscovado or light brown (soft) sugar

2 baking sheets

non-stick baking parchment

makes 10–12

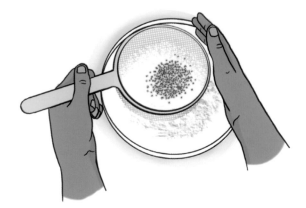

3 Place a large strainer (sieve) over a mixing bowl. Tip the flour, baking powder, spices, and salt into the strainer and sift them into the bowl.

4 Add the butter and then pick up small amounts of butter and flour and rub them together between your thumb and fingertips. Keep picking up more of the mixture and rubbing it together. In this way, the butter gradually gets mixed into the flour.

5 When the mixture starts to look like sand and there are no lumps of butter, add the sugar and mix it in with your fingers.

6 Now add the egg yolk and syrup mixture and mix it with a wooden spoon until the dough starts to clump together.

7 Sprinkle a little flour on your work surface and tip the mixture on top. Knead it gently to form the dough into a smooth ball.

8 Flatten the dough into a disc, put it in a sealable food bag, or wrap it in plastic wrap (clingfilm), and chill it in the refrigerator for 1–2 hours. You are now ready to roll out the dough.

Tip
Why not freeze some cookie dough to use at a later date? Thaw it overnight in the refrigerator before rolling out.

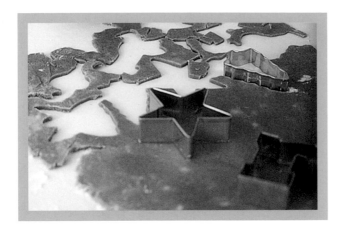

9 Line two baking sheets with baking parchment. Sprinkle a little flour on a clean work surface. Using a rolling pin, roll out the dough to a thickness of about ⅛ in. (3–4 mm). Stamp out shapes with cookie cutters. Gather up any scraps of cookie dough, knead very lightly to bring together into a ball, and roll out again to stamp out more cookies. Chill in the refrigerator for a further 15 minutes.

10 Arrange the shapes on the prepared baking sheets. Ask an adult to help you put the baking sheets on the middle shelf of the oven. Bake for 10–12 minutes until pale golden. Remove from the oven and leave the cookies to cool on the baking sheets before transferring to a wire rack to cool completely.

Spice up your COOKIES!

Vanilla cake

This cake recipe can be used for most of the cake projects in this book. Each project tells you which size of cake to make. For some of the projects you need to make two quantities of cake batter. If you try and put all the ingredients in together there will be too much for you to mix, so make the two cakes separately. Get all the ingredients ready for both cakes, make one cake and while that is cooking make the other one. You can make the cakes by yourself, mixing everything by hand, but it will be much quicker with an electric mixer. You must always ask an adult to help before you use a mixer.

Small Cake
You will need

This will make a 7-in. (18-cm) round cake. It needs to cook for 25 minutes.

1 stick (125 g) unsalted butter, at room temperature

½ cup (125 g) superfine (caster) sugar

2 large (UK medium) eggs, beaten

½ teaspoon vanilla extract

1 cup plus 2 tablespoons (125 g) all-purpose (plain) flour

2 teaspoons baking powder

2 tablespoons milk, at room temperature

Medium Cake
You will need

This will make an 8-in. (20-cm) round cake. It needs to cook for 30 minutes.

1½ sticks (175 g) unsalted butter, at room temperature

1 cup (175 g) superfine (caster) sugar

3 large (UK medium) eggs, beaten

1 teaspoon vanilla extract

1½ cups (175 g) all-purpose (plain) flour

3 teaspoons baking powder

3 tablespoons milk, at room temperature

Large Cake
You will need

This will make a 9-in. (23-cm) round cake. It needs to cook for 35–40 minutes.

2 sticks (250 g) unsalted butter, at room temperature

1¼ cups (250 g) superfine (caster) sugar

4 large (UK medium) eggs, beaten

1 teaspoon vanilla extract

2¼ cups (250 g) all-purpose (plain) flour

4 teaspoons baking powder

3–4 tablespoons milk, at room temperature

Lovely and light, the perfect sponge

1 Preheat the oven. Ask an adult to turn the oven on to 350°F (180°C) Gas 4 so it will be hot by the time you are ready to bake.

2 Prepare your cake pan. First read the project and find out which size of cake you need to make and which size pan. Find the correct pan and place it on some baking parchment. Draw around it and cut out the parchment circle. Scoop a little soft butter onto a paper towel and rub this all over the inside of the pan. Put the parchment circle into the base of the pan and leave it to one side.

3 Put the soft butter and sugar into a large mixing bowl and beat with a wooden spoon until the butter is soft, creamy, and pale (if an adult is helping, you could use an electric beater).

4 Break the eggs into a small bowl and remove any pieces of shell. Beat the eggs with a fork until the yolks have broken up and the mixture is a bit frothy.

5 Add a little egg to the creamed butter mixture and beat with the wooden spoon until the egg is all blended in. Then add a little more egg and beat again. Add a small sprinkle of flour if the mixture looks as though it is starting to separate (becoming bitty rather than smooth). Keep adding the egg until it is all used up and scrape any mixture down from the sides with a spatula.

6 Add the vanilla extract and stir it into the mixture.

7 Sift the flour and baking powder together into a separate bowl.

Tip

Remember to follow one type of measurement only. Either use cups and sticks which is the first type of measurement or follow the measurements in brackets and use a weighing scale and a measuring pitcher (jug).

8 Add half the flour to the mixture and fold it in. To fold, use a metal spoon to cut through the mixture in a gentle figure of eight. Don't beat or over-stir it—gentle folding traps air into the mixture and will make the cake lovely and light. When the half the flour is mixed in, add the second half and do the same folding.

9 Add the milk and fold it in. Your mixture should be smooth and drop from the spoon when you lift it.
If it is still very stiff add another spoonful and fold again.

Safety Tip
Always remember to put on oven mitts before you put something into the oven, as well as when you take it out.

10 Pour the batter into the cake pan, scraping the bowl with a soft spatula to get out all the mixture. Smooth out the surface with the spatula.

11 Put on oven mitts and ask an adult to help you put the cake in the oven. Check how long it will take for the size of cake you have baked, and set a timer.

12 When the time is up, check the cake through the oven door. It should have risen high in the pan and be a golden color. If it doesn't look done, leave it for a few minutes longer. Put on oven mitts. Ask an adult to help you to take it out. If it is ready, it will be have shrunk away from the side of the pan and when you press it with a finger it will spring back up. An extra test is to push a metal skewer into the center. If it comes out clean, the cake is cooked. If it is covered with sticky mix, it needs a bit longer in the oven. Leave the cake to cool in the pan for 5–10 minutes.

chapter 2

Decorating Techniques

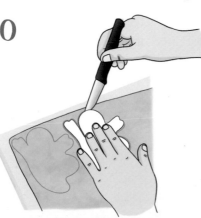

Making cookie templates

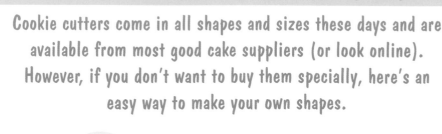

Cookie cutters come in all shapes and sizes these days and are available from most good cake suppliers (or look online). However, if you don't want to buy them specially, here's an easy way to make your own shapes.

You will need

....

white paper

templates on pages 124–125

pencil

scissors

thin cardstock (a cereal box is ideal)

glue stick

1 Choose which cookie shape you want to use from the templates on pages 124–125 and photocopy or trace it onto a piece of white paper. Alternatively, you can use one of your own shapes or look online for some fun templates.

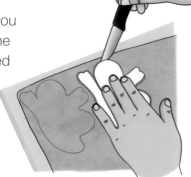

2 If you are making lots of cookies, you will be using the same template lots of times so you may want to glue the paper shape onto something sturdier, like the cardstock from a cereal box, to give it some strength.

3 Use the scissors to cut around the template.

4 Roll out the cookie dough on a large board so that you don't scratch your work surface when you cut out the cookies. Now place the template on top of your rolled out cookie dough and cut around it with a small, sharp knife. Always place the template as close to the edge as possible, and the next one you cut as close as possible to the one before. That way you can cut out lots of cookies before you need to roll out the dough again.

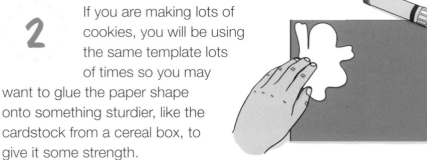

Tip

Cookie dough can be quite delicate when it comes out of the oven. Transfer the cookies carefully to try to avoid thin parts breaking off.

5 Use a metal spatula to transfer the shapes to your prepared baking sheet. Cutting cookie dough by hand does mean you sometimes get a few rough edges so use your fingertips to gently smooth the edges.

6 Gather up the trimmings, roll them into a ball, and cut more shapes as before. The cookies are now ready to bake!

DESIGN your own cookies!

Tinting icing

If you want a nice smooth finish to your cakes and cookies, you can use fondant icing. You can get it in different colors, but it's often better to buy white fondant and tint your own.

Tint the icing using food coloring pastes or gels. Get them from specialist shops or online. Liquid food coloring is available from supermarkets. You only need to add a few drops at a time to your icing—be very careful not to pour more than that in, as the color will be too strong and the liquid will turn your icing runny. Whether you are tinting fondant icing or buttercream, it is best to color it in one batch, otherwise you may end up with different shades.

Tinting fondant icing

1 Push your finger into the fondant to make a small hole. Use a wooden skewer or toothpick to add tiny amounts of food coloring paste or carefully add one or two drops at a time of liquid food coloring to the fondant icing.

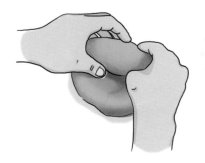

2 Knead the fondant so that the color is evenly mixed without any streaks. If you want the color to be deeper, add a little more coloring and knead again. Keep doing this until you have the color you want.

3 If you want to color a large amount of fondant, a good tip is to color a small of ball fondant to a darker shade than you need and then knead this into a larger amount of fondant. This is much easier than trying to knead a small amount of color evenly through one large amount.

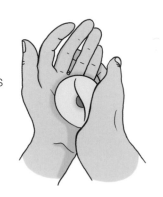

4 Another fun way to color your fondant is to create a marbled effect. You can do this by kneading together two balls of fondant in different colors, but stop before they are mixed all the way through. When you roll it out, you will see a lovely marbled pattern.

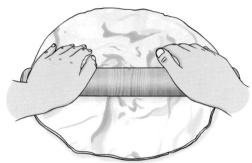

Tinting sugar icing and buttercream frosting

Use a wooden skewer or toothpick to add tiny amounts of food coloring paste or add just a drop or two of liquid food coloring to the frosting or icing and mix it in thoroughly with a spoon. If you want the color to be deeper, add a little more coloring and stir again. Keep doing this until you have the color you want.

Mixing colors

It is possible to make different colors by mixing food coloring liquids. Mix the color in a separate bowl before adding it to your icing and test the color first to check that you have the right shade.

Here are a few color combinations:

● + ● = ● Red + blue = purple

● + ● = ● Red + green = brown

● + ● = ● Red + yellow = orange

● + ● = ● Blue + yellow = green

Covering a cake with buttercream

Using buttercream is the easiest way to decorate a big cake. It is really good for cupcakes too. Buttercream is easy to make and can be flavored in lots of different ways and colored to fit with your design. Also, If you want to cover a cake with fondant icing (see opposite), you'll need to cover it with buttercream first, to create a layer for the fondant to stick to.

1 Prepare your buttercream (see page 27)—if you have made it in advance and kept it in the refrigerator, you may need to beat it lightly with a wooden spoon to soften it. Put your cake on a cake stand or plate—ideally one that you can turn to get to all sides of the cake. Start by dolloping a large spoonful of buttercream onto the top of your cake.

2 Use a palette knife to spread the buttercream evenly over the top of the cake, making sure you go right to the edges. Use the palette knife to even out the buttercream, scraping any excess buttercream back into the bowl.

Tip

If you are covering a cake with buttercream before adding a layer of fondant icing, you only need a thin layer of buttercream. It's also a good idea to put the buttercream-covered cake in the refrigerator for 30 minutes before you add the fondant so it is nice and firm.

3 Now start adding buttercream to the sides of the cake. Don't try to add it all in one go— work gradually around the sides of the cake, using the palette knife to cover the sides and turning the plate or board as you go.

Covering a cake with fondant

Fondant icing is great for decorating both cakes and cookies as it gives a lovely smooth finish. Using it to cover cookies is really easy as you can just roll it and stamp out shapes with your cookie cutter. When covering a cake, you'll need to work with a much larger piece—this can be quite tricky, but is fun to do!

1 Get everything ready: make sure your work surface is really clean and dry and there are no stray crumbs that might get stuck in your icing! To work out how big a circle (or rectangle) of fondant you need, hold a piece of string at the base and take it up and across the cake top and down the other side. Cut the string a little longer than this length and keep for later. Now cover your cake with buttercream (see opposite), otherwise the fondant won't stick to the cake. Pop it into the refrigerator while you roll the fondant.

2 Have your buttercream-covered cake to hand, as well as your rolling pin. Lightly dust your work surface with confectioners' (icing) sugar.

3 Unwrap the fondant and knead for a couple of minutes to soften it. If it feels very stiff, you can pop it in the microwave for about 10 seconds. Take your rolling pin and start rolling. Don't try to squash the icing flat—the trick is to roll gently and firmly, pushing the rolling pin away from you to stretch the icing and turning the icing to make sure it isn't sticking to the work surface. Keep lifting the edges to check and add more sugar if it is. You may need to dust your rolling pin with sugar too if that begins sticking to the icing. Try to get it an even thickness, ideally about ⅛ in. (3 mm) thick.

4 When you have rolled out the fondant, use the piece of string you cut in step 1 to check it is large enough in all directions. You are now ready to cover your cake—you may need some help with this step. Place the buttercream-covered cake near to you and dust your hands with confectioners' (icing) sugar. Carefully lift the fondant icing by sliding both hands under it, taking care not to tear any holes in it. Draping it over the rolling pin can help to lift it. Position it over the cake and then smooth over the top—this will get rid of any trapped air bubbles and make the icing stick to the buttercream on the top of the cake.

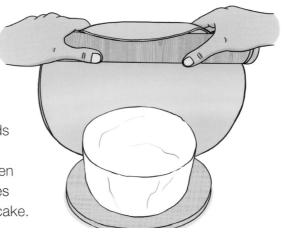

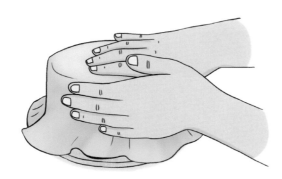

5 Now smooth your hands down the sides of the cake, opening out any "pleats" and pressing the fondant gently into the cake. You should have a "skirt" of icing at the bottom of the cake.

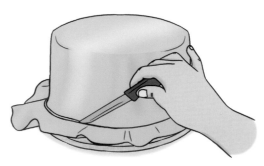

Tip

Take care with fondant icing because it can dry out, which will lead to cracks forming, so always keep your icing wrapped in plastic wrap (clingfilm) until you are ready to use it.

6 Now all you have to do is trim the excess fondant away at the bottom edge of the cake. Use a small knife to trim the icing, making sure you don't cut too close to the edge of the cake. Keep these offcuts in an airtight container to use on other cakes!

Piping

Piping is a brilliant technique to learn as it can be used to add decoration to cakes and cookies in lots of different ways. Use a piping bag fitted with a star tip and filled with buttercream to create rosettes or flowers, and use a small round tip for flooding cookies (see below) and "drawing" on patterns. You'll need to keep practicing to become good at piping, but even if your first attempts don't look brilliant they will still taste good!

Piping bags and tips

• Disposable plastic piping bags in various sizes are available from most supermarkets. These are really easy to use: you just drop your chosen piping tip into the bag and then snip off enough of the end of the bag so that the tip fits snugly.

• You can also find reusable nylon piping bags from specialist cake shops and decorating suppliers. They are a little sturdier and you don't need to snip off the end. They can be rinsed and washed inside out in hot water—always make sure they are completely dry before putting them away.

• Piping tips (or nozzles) are little conical tubes that fit into the end of your piping bag and are available in lots of different shapes and sizes, from fine writing tips to large star or rosette shapes. You can often find good-value sets that include a reusable bag plus a set of piping tips.

How to fill a piping bag

1

Drop your chosen piping tip into the piping bag. If you are using a disposable bag, use scissors to snip off just enough to make the tip fit snugly.

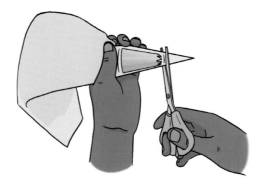

2 Put the bag in a tall glass and fold the top of the bag over the rim of the glass. The glass will support the bag and make it easier to fill.

3 Spoon the buttercream, frosting, or icing into the bag, making sure you don't fill it more than two-thirds full. If you have small hands and when you are learning this technique, it is easier to use less icing so the bag is not too big and heavy.

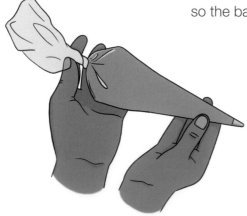

4 Unfold the bag from the rim of the glass and twist the top to push the mixture down to the tip end, pushing out any air pockets, then twist it again to stop the mixture escaping from the top.

5 Gently squeeze the bag so that the mixture fills the nozzle. Have a little practice on a board before you start, so you can get used to the flow of the icing and work out how hard you need to squeeze. You are now ready to pipe!

How to pipe

1 You need a firm and steady hand for smooth and even piping so hold the bag with both hands, with your stronger hand holding the top of the bag (your right hand if you are right-handed). Your other hand should be at the bottom, near the tip—this is your guiding hand.

2 Holding the bag as upright as possible, squeeze the bag gently, using even pressure so that the mixture comes out in a smooth flow. For stiff mixtures, such as buttercream or chocolate fudge frosting, you may need to squeeze quite firmly. Royal icing should flow quite easily—if you are finding it difficult to pipe your icing, you may need to remove the icing from the bag and thin it with a little water.

3 To pipe a star or rosette decoration (see the Sunflower cookies on page 72), you may need to practice a little. Position the tip above the cake or cookie, squeeze gently to form a star, then release the pressure as you lift the bag away.

4 If you are piping lots of details, make sure you stop from time to time to push the mixture evenly down the bag and twist the top of the bag again.

5 If you still have lots of mixture in your piping bag when you have finished, simply squeeze it back into the bowl, cover with plastic wrap (clingfilm) and keep for another decorating project!

Tip

If you are piping chocolate, for example for the Black and white cookies on page 78, just remember that chocolate hardens as it cools, so you may need to remove hardened chocolate from the tip of the piping bag as you work. With chocolate, it's best to work quickly!

Flooding cookies

Some of the cookies in this book use a technique called "flooding". This involves creating an outline or "wall" of icing around the edge of the cookie, usually with royal icing. The area inside the "wall" is then filled with a slightly thinner royal icing. This gives the cookie a lovely smooth finish.

1 Fit a piping bag with a small round piping tip and then fill it with a small amount of royal icing in your chosen color (see page 29). Holding the bag with both hands and as vertically upright as possible, pipe an outline around the edge of your cookies. If your cookies have a cut-out shape in the middle, you may need to pipe another outline for the inner edge.

2 Once you have outlined all your cookies, squeeze any remaining royal icing back into the bowl. Now add a few drops of water, a little at a time, to make a slightly thinner icing. Don't make it too runny—to check, drag a knife through the royal icing and count how long it take for it to smooth over. It should be about 10 seconds—any less and the icing is too runny so you will need to add some confectioners' (icing) sugar to thicken it.

3 Now you are ready to "flood" the cookies by spreading icing up to the outlines. You can do this with a teaspoon or mini palette knife, or by putting the icing in a piping bag and squeezing onto the cookie. The icing should be runny enough that it fills up to the edges easily.

4 If you want to add sprinkles or edible glitter to the cookies, do this before the royal icing sets hard. Otherwise leave the cookies to one side for the icing to harden slightly for about 1 hour. You'll then be able to add any other piped details.

Making chocolate decorations

Professional chocolatiers (people who work with chocolate) "temper" chocolate, which is quite tricky to master! It means the melted chocolate keeps its structure and can be molded. But you can still do lots with chocolate without tempering it!

Chocolate-covered strawberries

There's something about chocolate and strawberries that everyone loves—and these are so pretty too! Think about other fruits you could dip—how about banana slices or kiwi fruit?

1 Gently rinse the strawberries in cold water and shake off the excess water. Leave the stalks and leaves on (you'll need these to dip the strawberries). The berries need to be completely dry before you dip them so set them aside on some paper towel.

You will need

2 cups (500 g) medium strawberries

6 oz. (175 g) bittersweet (dark) or white chocolate

1 teaspoon vegetable oil

baking sheet lined with non-stick baking parchment

makes about 24

2 Break the chocolate into pieces and put into a heatproof bowl with the vegetable oil. Ask an adult to help you set the bowl over a pan of barely simmering water, making sure that the bottom of the bowl doesn't touch the water. Stir until melted and smooth, then set aside to cool slightly.

3 Holding each strawberry by its stalk, dip the lower half into the melted chocolate. Hold the strawberry over the bowl of chocolate for a few seconds, to allow the excess chocolate to drip back into the bowl.

4 Place on the lined baking tray and repeat until you have dipped all the strawberries. Put the tray in the refrigerator for about 30 minutes until the chocolate hardens.

Making chocolate curls

This is super easy to do and doesn't even involve any melting or heating!

1 Take a block or large piece of chocolate—bittersweet (dark) chocolate will give better results than softer milk or white chocolate. Don't use chocolate straight from the refrigerator as it will be too hard.

2 Use a vegetable peeler to make your curls—just scrape it along the edge of your chocolate bar. Carefully put the curls into a small bowl.

3 Cover the bowl and refrigerate until needed. They will be quite delicate so take care when taking them out and putting them on your cake.

Piping with chocolate

Once you have got the hang of using a piping bag (see page 43), you will be able to create all sorts of lovely patterns with melted chocolate! Remember that chocolate will harden and set the longer you leave it, so you'll need to work quite quickly.

1 Melt the chocolate as for the chocolate-covered strawberries on page 45 (but you don't need to add any oil to the bowl). Stir until melted and smooth, then set aside to cool slightly.

2 Put the melted chocolate into your piping bag (see page 41). Just put in a little bit or it will harden before you have used it up. Hold the top of the piping bag with your strong hand and use the other hand to guide the tip and squeeze gently. Start piping designs onto the baking parchment—it might take a few goes before you get them right! Try making hearts, swirls, or just random squiggles. You could even have a go at writing your name!

3 When you have finished put the baking sheet into the freezer for about 5 minutes, or until the chocolate has hardened. Carefully peel the chocolate shapes off the parchment paper and transfer to an airtight container (you could also use a palette knife to lift them off the paper). Keep them in the refrigerator until you are ready to decorate your cake.

You will need

½ cup (100 g) bittersweet (dark chocolate) chips

piping bag fitted with fine writing tip (nozzle)

baking sheet lined with non-stick baking parchment

Tip

If you want to make lots of the same shape or you want very accurate designs, make a template and draw around it on the parchment. Then turn the parchment over. You can still see your pencil shape and can pipe over the lines. This won't work for writing as it will be the wrong way round!

Making sugar flowers

What could be prettier than a cake or cookie decorated with sugar flowers? White flower and modeling paste can be colored and rolled in the same way as fondant icing, but is better for molding and shaping more delicate shapes like flowers as it sets harder. You'll need to make these a couple of days before using to give them time to completely dry out. They would look lovely on top of a cake covered with white fondant (see page 39).

You will need

8 oz. (225 g) white flower and modeling paste (available from supermarkets)

yellow food coloring paste

orange food coloring paste

pink food coloring paste

red food coloring paste

confectioners' (icing) sugar, for dusting

assorted small flower-shaped cutters

embossing tools (optional)

teaspoons and dessertspoons

makes about 24

1 Decide how many colors you want to make—remember that you can make more than one shade of the same color by gradually adding more coloring. Tint the modeling paste using the food coloring pastes (see page 36 for more on tinting).

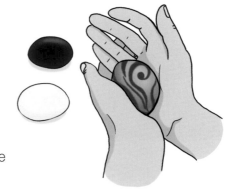

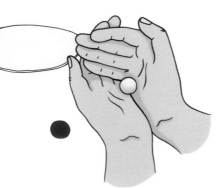

2 Lightly dust a clean work surface with confectioners' (icing) sugar. Roll the modeling paste out as evenly as you can— ideally about ⅛ in. (3 mm) thick. Cut off tiny pieces of paste and roll them into balls for the centers of the flowers. Put on a plate to dry.

Make enough to fill a GARDEN!

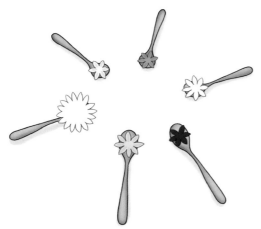

3 Use different flower-shaped cutters to stamp out flowers in lots of shapes and sizes. If you have an embossing tool, you can use it to add some details, otherwise use a wooden skewer (or leave them plain).

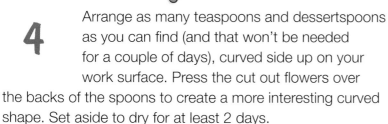

4 Arrange as many teaspoons and dessertspoons as you can find (and that won't be needed for a couple of days), curved side up on your work surface. Press the cut out flowers over the backs of the spoons to create a more interesting curved shape. Set aside to dry for at least 2 days.

5 When you are ready to add these to your cake (or cookies), mix a small amount of confectioners' (icing) sugar with a tiny amount of water to make a gloopy icing. Use a paintbrush or a toothpick to dab a small amount of this icing onto the underside of each flower and "glue" them onto your cake. Stick the tiny flower centers to the flowers with a dot of icing.

Tip
If you are looking in cake decorating shops or online, you may come across plunger cutters. These are little cutters that have a little plunger at the top, which will push your shape out of the cutter (without you having to use your fingers and smudge it!). Some of them will also emboss a little pattern on your shape.

making sugar flowers 49

Making sugar mice ☺ ☺ ○

Make these little mice at least one day before you want to use them to decorate a cake, to give them plenty of time to dry out. The recipe makes enough for lots of mice—just think how cute they'll look nestled up together or chasing each other around the edge of the cake.

You will need

....

1 large (UK medium) egg

1 teaspoon lemon juice

3¼–4 cups (400–500 g) confectioners' (icing) sugar, sifted

pink food coloring paste

small chocolate sprinkles

kitchen string

wooden skewer

baking sheet lined with non-stick baking parchment

makes 12

1 First separate the egg white from the yolk. To do this, carefully break the egg onto a plate, place an egg cup over the yolk, and let the white slide off into a clean mixing bowl. You do not need the yolk for this recipe, so put it into another bowl to use for something else.

2 Whisk the egg white with a balloon whisk until foamy and then stir in the lemon juice.

3 Gradually add the confectioners' (icing) sugar and stir in with a wooden spoon. When it starts to feel like a really stiff dough, lightly dust your work surface with confectioners' (icing) sugar and tip the mixture onto it. Use your hands to squish the mixture together and knead it until it feels softer and a bit more like modeling clay.

Tip

Make sure your hands are really clean and dry before you start. Cool hands are best as the sugar mixture will start to get sticky if your hands are too warm!

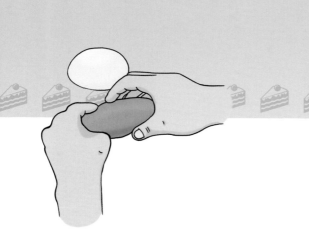

4 To make half the mice pink and half the mice white, divide the mixture in two. Add a tiny bit of pink food coloring to one half and knead it until all the color is evenly mixed in. Add a tiny bit more coloring if you want a stronger color.

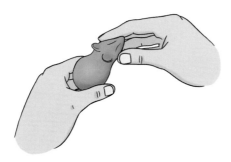

5 Break off a walnut-sized piece of mixture and roll into a cone shape. Pinch little ears on top of the narrow end. Squeeze the narrow end into a nose.

6 Press two chocolate sprinkles into the face below the ears to make the eyes. Cut a length of string about 1–1½ in. (2–4 cm) and push it into the round end of the mouse to make the tail.

7 Use a wooden skewer to dab a tiny amount of pink food coloring on the end of the nose. Put the mouse on the prepared baking sheet and then repeat with the remaining mixture to make 12 mice. Leave the mice to dry out for at least 12 hours before you serve them.

Cute little PINK mice!

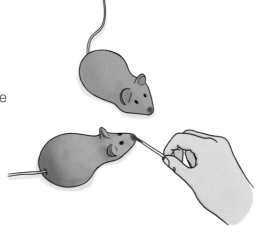

chapter 3

Creative Cookies

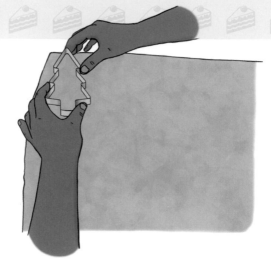

2 Roll the dough out to a thickness of ⅛ in. (3 mm) on a lightly floured work surface. Using the Christmas tree cookie cutters, carefully stamp out shapes and arrange them on the prepared baking sheets. Gather up any scraps of cookie dough, knead lightly into a ball, and roll out again to stamp more cookies. Refrigerate for 15 minutes and ask an adult to help you preheat the oven to 350°F (180°C) Gas 4.

3 Ask an adult to help you put the baking sheets in the preheated oven. Bake for about 10–12 minutes, or until the cookies are pale golden and firm to the touch. Leave the cookies to cool on the baking sheets before transferring to a wire rack to cool completely.

4 While the cookies are cooling, make the sugar icing. Place a strainer (sieve) over a bowl and sift the confectioners' (icing) sugar into the bowl. Add 2–4 tablespoons of warm water, mixing it in quickly until the icing is smooth. You don't want the icing to be too runny, or it will just run off your cookies, so add the water a little at a time until you get the right consistency. If you make a mistake and it is too runny, just add more sugar, a little at a time, until you have got it right.

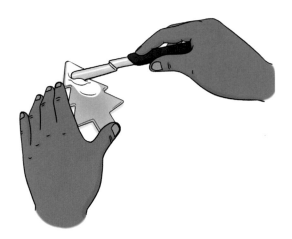

5 When the cookies are cold, use a small palette knife to carefully spread the icing over one cookie at a time, trying to keep it as neat as possible.

6 Use the writing icing tubes to pipe tinsel across the cookie. Position the sugar balls and edible sprinkles over the top to look like tree ornaments.

Tip

The sugar icing will set quite quickly, so decorate your cookies one at a time, otherwise the icing will set before the sprinkles can stick to it.

4 Make the Royal Icing. Decide how many colors of icing you need and divide the icing into as many bowls. Tint each one a different color: use a wooden skewer or toothpick to add tiny amounts of food coloring paste or add just a drop or two of liquid food coloring to the icing and mix it in thoroughly with a spoon. If you want the color to be deeper, add a little more coloring and stir again.

5 Choose which colour you want to start with and spoon a small amount into the piping bag. Holding it over the bowl, squeeze the icing down the bag until it reaches the tip. Pipe an outline all around the edge of all the cookies that have the same color background and set aside to harden for about 5 minutes. Don't leave any gaps! It is quite tricky to keep the line from wobbling around—you will get better with practice.

Tip

If you don't have cookie cutters in the shapes you need, you could make your own templates (see page 34).

6 Now you need to "flood" the area inside the border with the same color icing (see page 44). Add a few drops of water to the royal icing in the bowl to make it slightly thinner. Use a teaspoon or mini palette knife to spread icing over the surface of the cookie, inside the border.

7 You will need to let the background dry and harden slightly before you pipe any lines on top of the flooded icing. While it is drying, work on the background colors of other critters. When you have finished all the backgrounds then you can start on the details of the first ones you iced. Allow to set before eating.

FLUTTERBY, butterfly, creep and crawl!

Easter bunny cookies

These cute bunny cookies make wonderful gifts at Easter or can brighten up the tea table at a springtime birthday party. You can buy bunny cookie cutters from bakeware stores or online.

You will need

....

1 quantity Vanilla Cookie dough (see page 14)

1 lb. (450 g) ready-to-roll white fondant icing

confectioners' (icing) sugar

pink and black writing icing

1 yd (1 m) each of blue and pink gingham ribbon

2 baking sheets

non-stick baking parchment

bunny cookie cutters (2 shapes if possible)

makes 12–18, depending on size

1 Make the Vanilla Cookie dough and chill in the refrigerator for 1–2 hours. Meanwhile, cut pieces of non-stick baking parchment to cover the baking sheets and ask an adult to turn the oven on to 400°F (200°C) Gas 6.

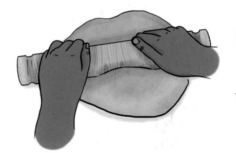

2 Sprinkle a clean work surface with flour and roll out the cookie dough until it is about ¼ in. (5 mm) thick.

3 Use your bunny cutters to cut out as many bunnies as you can, cutting them as close together as possible. When you have cut out the first batch, gather all the trimmings together, roll them out again, and cut some more shapes.

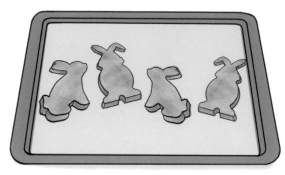

4 Lay all the cookies on the baking sheets and ask an adult to help you put them into the preheated oven for 12–16 minutes, until the cookies are golden. Ask an adult to take them out of the oven and let them cool on a wire rack.

5 To decorate the bunnies, first make a little "edible glue" by putting 2 tablespoons of confectioners' (icing) sugar in a cup and adding 2 tablespoons of warm water. Stir together.

6 Sprinkle a little confectioners' (icing) sugar onto a clean work surface. Roll out the fondant icing (see page 39) until it is about ¼ in. (5 mm) thick. Each time you roll the icing, lift it, turn it a little, and sprinkle on a little more confectioners' (icing) sugar to stop it sticking to the work surface. Sprinkle a little confectioners' (icing) sugar onto the rolling pin too, if that sticks.

Tip
When you cut cookies, always start at the edge of the cookie dough not the middle. That way you will squeeze more cookies in before you have to gather up the dough and roll it out again.

7 Brush a little of your "sugar glue" onto the first cookie. Use the cookie cutter to cut out an icing shape to match the bunny and carefully stick it on. Do the same for the rest of the bunnies.

8 Use writing icing to draw on eyes, noses, tails, and whiskers. To make fluffy tails, squeeze lots of dots close together. When the writing icing has set, loosely tie a piece of ribbon into a bow around each bunny's neck.

Cute BUNNIES for Easter!

Sunflower cookies

Brighten up a winter's day with these colorful cookies or celebrate summer, when it comes, with a cookie version of the real thing. You use two different types of frosting for these—fondant and royal icing.

You will need

1 quantity Vanilla Cookie dough (see page 14)

8–10 oz. (225–300 g) white ready-to-roll fondant icing

yellow food coloring paste

½ quantity Royal Icing (see page 29)

black food coloring paste

confectioners' (icing) sugar

4–5-in. (10–12-cm) sunflower-shaped cookie cutter

2 baking sheets

non-stick baking parchment

small piping bag fitted with a small star-shaped tip (nozzle)

makes about 12, depending on size

1 Make the Vanilla Cookie dough and chill in the refrigerator for 1–2 hours. Meanwhile, cut pieces of non-stick baking parchment to cover the baking sheets.

2 Roll the dough out to a thickness of ⅛ in. (3 mm) on a lightly floured work surface. Using the cookie cutters, carefully stamp out shapes and arrange them on the prepared baking sheets.

3 Gather together the scraps of the dough and re-roll to make more shapes. Refrigerate for 15 minutes and ask an adult to preheat the oven to 350°F (180°C) Gas 4.

4 Ask an adult to help you put the cookies on the middle shelf of the preheated oven to bake for about 12 minutes, or until golden. Leave to cool on the trays for 5 minutes before transferring to a wire rack to cool completely.

5 Tint the fondant icing yellow (see page 36 for how to tint) using the yellow food coloring paste and the royal icing black using the black food coloring paste.

6 Make a little edible sugar "glue" by putting 2 tablespoons confectioners' (icing) sugar in a cup and adding 2 tablespoons warm water. Stir them together.

YUMMY, sunny sunflowers

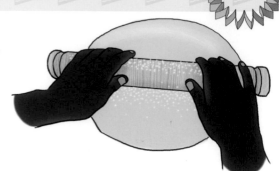

7 Lightly dust a work surface with confectioners' (icing) sugar. Roll out the yellow fondant icing very thinly—about 1/16 in. (2 mm).

8 Lightly brush the top of one cookie with edible "glue." Then using the sunflower cookie cutter again, stamp out a flower from the fondant icing to match the cookie but leave the cookie cutter in place.

9 Carefully lift the cookie cutter (with the fondant flower still inside) and position it on top of the cookie. Gently press out the fondant flower and smooth down with your fingers.

10 Fill the piping bag with the black royal icing and pipe rosettes into the middle of each sunflower (see page 43 for help on piping).

11 Put the cookies on a plate and set aside to allow the royal icing to set before eating.

Glittery ghosts

These ghost popsicles (lollipops) made from cookie dough are ideal for a Halloween party. Make them in ghoulish white and green and add lots of glitter for some spooky sparkle.

1 Make the Vanilla Cookie dough and chill in the refrigerator for 1–2 hours. Meanwhile, cut pieces of non-stick baking parchment to cover the baking sheets.

You will need

....

1 quantity Vanilla Cookie dough (see page 14)

1 quantity Royal Icing (see page 29)

black writing icing

green food coloring paste

edible glitter

2 baking sheets

non-stick baking parchment

ghost cookie cutter

small piping bag fitted with a fine writing tip (nozzle)

12 popsicle (lollipop) sticks

makes 16

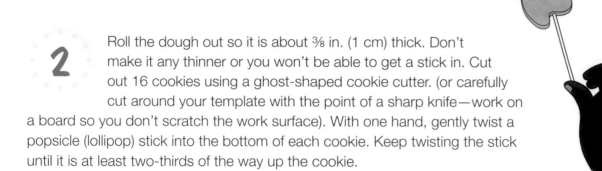

2 Roll the dough out so it is about ⅜ in. (1 cm) thick. Don't make it any thinner or you won't be able to get a stick in. Cut out 16 cookies using a ghost-shaped cookie cutter. (or carefully cut around your template with the point of a sharp knife—work on a board so you don't scratch the work surface). With one hand, gently twist a popsicle (lollipop) stick into the bottom of each cookie. Keep twisting the stick until it is at least two-thirds of the way up the cookie.

3 Carefully turn the cookie over. Roll a small sausage of cookie dough and attach it to the top of the stick where it meets the cookie. This will strengthen the cookie and will disappear when it is baked.

4 Place the cookies on the prepared baking sheets and chill in the refrigerator for 30 minutes. Meanwhile, ask an adult to help you preheat the oven to 400°F (200°C) Gas 6.

5 Ask an adult to help you bake the cookies on the middle shelf of the oven for 12–16 minutes, or until the cookies are golden. Transfer to a wire rack to cool.

Tip
If you don't have a ghost cookie cutter, you can make a template to cut around (see page 34).

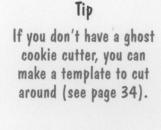

6 Prepare the Royal icing (see page 29). Divide the icing into two bowls and tint one of them pale green using the green food coloring paste (see page 37).

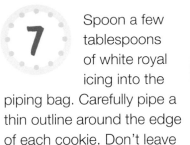

7 Spoon a few tablespoons of white royal icing into the piping bag. Carefully pipe a thin outline around the edge of each cookie. Don't leave any gaps! It is quite tricky to keep the line from wobbling around—you will get better with practice. Leave to dry for at least 5 minutes before flooding (see page 44) the middle: use a teaspoon to fill in the area inside the border with more white or green icing. Add a few drops of water to the royal icing in the bowl to make it slightly thinner before you start.

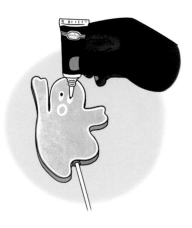

8 Put the cookies on some waxed (greaseproof) paper and sprinkle with edible glitter—you'll need to do this before the icing sets hard.

9 Finally, using white icing, pipe a circle for the mouth and 2 ovals for the eyes. Add a dot of black writing icing to each eye to finish the cookie.

Perfect for a **HALLOWEEN** party!

Black and white cookies

You will need

1⅓ cups (150 g) all-purpose (plain) flour, plus extra for dusting

⅓ cup (40 g) unsweetened cocoa powder

½ teaspoon baking powder

½ teaspoon baking soda (bicarbonate of soda)

pinch of salt

1 large (UK medium) egg

1 teaspoon vanilla extract

1 stick (125 g) unsalted butter, softened

1 cup plus 2 tablespoons (200 g) superfine (caster) sugar

To decorate

9½ oz. (275 g) bittersweet (dark) chocolate, chopped

2 tablespoons sunflower oil

3½ oz. (100 g) white chocolate, chopped

round cookie cutters

2 baking sheets

non-stick baking parchment

small piping bag fitted with a fine writing tip (nozzle)

wooden skewer

makes about 16

These cookies are easy to make but their feathered frosting looks very sophisticated. Have fun being artistic with plenty of swirls and flourishes of white chocolate on a shiny dark chocolate glaze. We have made round cookies but you could make them in different shapes.

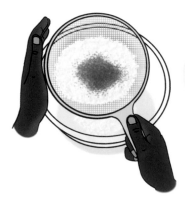

1 Sift together the flour, cocoa powder, baking powder, baking soda (bicarbonate of soda), and salt into a mixing bowl.

2 Break the egg into a small bowl and remove any pieces of shell. Add the vanilla extract and beat with a fork until the yolk has broken up and the mixture is a bit frothy.

3 Put the butter and sugar into another large mixing bowl and beat with a wooden spoon until light and creamy (or ask an adult to help you use an electric beater). Add the egg and mix again well. Finally add the sifted dry ingredients and mix until smooth.

SWIRL, swirl away!

4 Squash everything together into a ball and knead lightly for a very short time until you have a smooth dough. Flatten it into a disk, wrap in plastic wrap (clingfilm), and refrigerate for a couple of hours until it is very firm.

5 When you are nearly ready to start baking, ask an adult to help you preheat the oven to 350°F (180°C) Gas 4. Cut some rectangles of non-stick baking parchment to fit your baking sheets.

6 Dust the work surface with flour and roll out the chilled cookie dough to a thickness of about ⅛ in. (3 mm). Using the cookie cutters, carefully stamp out rounds. Arrange them on the prepared baking sheets. Gather together the scraps of the dough and re-roll to make more rounds.

7 Ask an adult to put the baking sheets on the middle shelf of the preheated oven for 12–15 minutes, or until crisp. Leave to cool on the sheets for a couple of minutes before transferring the cookies—still on the parchment—to a wire rack to cool completely. While the cookies are cooling, make the dark chocolate glaze.

8 Put the bittersweet (dark) chocolate and sunflower oil in a heatproof bowl. Ask an adult to help you put the bowl over a pan of barely simmering water, making sure the bottom of the bowl doesn't touch the water. Stir very carefully until melted. Take it off the stove but leave the bowl over the pan of hot water so that it doesn't get too cold and set.

9 Now put the white chocolate pieces into a separate heatproof bowl and melt in the same way. Take it off the stove but leave the bowl over the pan of hot water so that it doesn't go too cold and set.

10 Use a spoon to pour some of the dark chocolate glaze over each cookie. Spread the glaze neatly over the cookie, just to the edge, with the back of the spoon (or you could use a mini palette knife).

11 Ask an adult to help you put a little of the melted white chocolate into the piping bag. Working on just a few cookies at a time (the white chocolate will set quite quickly), pipe dots of white chocolate over the dark chocolate glaze.

12 Using the point of the wooden skewer, drag the white chocolate into the chocolate glaze to create a swirly effect—this is called "feathering." Refill the piping bag and repeat with the remaining cookies. Try to let the chocolate set before eating!

Stained glass cookies

These cookies have crunchy, sweet, transparent centers that look like stained glass. Hold them up and let the light shine through them in jewel-like colors. Making the centers involves some fun candy-crushing too!

You will need

....

1 quantity Vanilla Cookie dough (page 14)

all-purpose (plain) flour, for rolling out

1 bag fruit-flavored hard candies

2 baking sheets

non-stick baking parchment

selection of shaped cookie cutters in different sizes— simple shapes like stars or flowers work best

strong plastic food bags

makes about 24

1 Make the Vanilla Cookie dough and chill in the refrigerator for 1–2 hours. Meanwhile, cut pieces of non-stick baking parchment to cover the baking sheets.

2 Roll the dough out to a thickness of ⅛ in. (3 mm) on a lightly floured work surface. Using the cookie cutters, carefully stamp out shapes and arrange them on the prepared baking sheets.

3 Using smaller cutters (it could be the same shape or a different one), cut out a shape in the center of each cookie. Gather together the scraps of the dough and re-roll to make more shapes. Refrigerate for 15 minutes and ask an adult to preheat the oven to 350°F (180°C) Gas 4.

4 Divide the hard candies into separate colors and pop into plastic food bags. Using a rolling pin, crush the candies into small pieces.

5 Take the stamped cookies out of the refrigerator. Carefully fill the empty space in the center of each cookie with the crushed candies in an even, thin layer and no thicker than the depth of the cookies.

6 Ask an adult to help you bake the cookies, one baking sheet at a time, on the middle shelf of the preheated oven for about 12 minutes, or until the cookies are pale golden and the candy has melted to fill the space. Let the cookies cool on the sheets until the "stained glass" has set.

Creative Cakes

Lemon cake with candies

You can go wild with the decorations for this one, using lots of different varieties and colors of candies. The key is to add all the sweet treats to the cake no more than 1–2 hours before serving, otherwise they might soften and bleed into the frosting.

You will need

1 quantity Large Lemon Cake (see page 26)

3 sticks (350 g) unsalted butter, softened

4 cups (600 g) confectioners' (icing) sugar

4 tablespoons lemon curd

assorted candies

2 x 8-in. (20-cm) round cake pans

non-stick baking parchment

serves 12

Tip

Why not arrange the candy to spell out someone's name, or their age if it is a birthday cake?

1 Ask an adult to help you turn the oven on to 350°F (180°C) Gas 4, so it will be hot by the time you are ready to bake. Put one of the round cake pans on the baking parchment and draw around it twice to make two circles. Cut them out. Scoop a little soft butter onto a paper towel and rub this all over the inside of the pans. Put the parchment circles into the bases of the pans and leave to one side.

2 Make the cake batter, following the instructions on pages 21–26, and spoon it evenly into the two pans. Ask an adult to help you put them onto the middle shelf of the oven for about 30 minutes. Leave the sponges to cool in the pans for about 10 minutes before turning out onto a wire rack. Turn them the right way up and leave to cool.

3 When the cakes are cold, slice each one in half horizontally to give four even layers (see page 32).

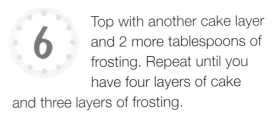

4 Make the frosting. Put the soft butter into a bowl and place a strainer (sieve) over the bowl. Add a few tablespoons of confectioners' (icing) sugar to the strainer and sift over the butter. Now beat the mixture together with a wooden spoon, then add a little more sugar and mix again. Keep going until all the sugar has been mixed in and the frosting is smooth and pale. Add the lemon curd and mix again until smooth.

5 Place one cake layer on a serving plate and spread with 2 big tablespoons of frosting.

6 Top with another cake layer and 2 more tablespoons of frosting. Repeat until you have four layers of cake and three layers of frosting.

7 Cover the top and sides of the cake with the remaining frosting, spreading it evenly with a palette knife.

8 Decorate the cake with a whole range of your favorite candies!

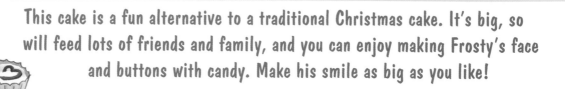

Frosty the snowman

This cake is a fun alternative to a traditional Christmas cake. It's big, so will feed lots of friends and family, and you can enjoy making Frosty's face and buttons with candy. Make his smile as big as you like!

You will need

....

1 quantity Medium Vanilla Cake (see page 21)

1 quantity Large Vanilla Cake (see page 21)

1 quantity Buttercream (see page 27)

red food coloring paste

2¼ cups (300 g) shredded (desiccated) coconut

1 large unfrosted cupcake (shop-bought or homemade)

1 plain licorice candy

dark chocolate chips

4 red sugar-coated candies

1¼ oz. (40 g) white ready-to-roll fondant icing

orange food coloring paste

2 short lengths of flaked chocolate

7-in. (18-cm) round cake pan, greased and base lined with non-stick baking parchment

9-in. (23-cm) round cake pan, greased and base lined with non-stick baking parchment

ribbon

serves 14

1 Using the recipe for Vanilla Cake on page 21, make one medium and one large cake. Remember to make these separately as you will have too much mix to make them both together. While the cakes are cooling, make the Buttercream (see page 27).

2 Now for decorating: take the buttercream and put 5 tablespoons into a small bowl. Tint this small amount red using the food coloring paste (see page 37).

3 Lay the cakes side by side on a big board (make sure they are cold). You may need to cut a thin layer off the tops of the cakes so they are flat and the same height (see page 32). This is quite tricky and you may need to ask an adult to help.

Don't eat all the candy!

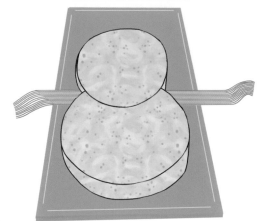

4 Take the smaller cake pan and hold it on top of the big cake where the snowman's head will be, overlapping the big cake by about 2 in. (5 cm). Use a skewer to draw around the pan, scratching the surface of the cake. With a sharp knife, carefully cut the leaf shape you have drawn out of the big cake. Keep this piece to make the hat.

5 Lay the ribbon horizontally on the board at the top of the big cake where Frosty's neck will be (this will be a scarf), before fitting the smaller cake into the curved space you have cut.

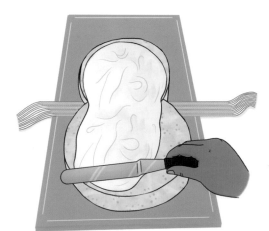

6 Cover the top and side of both of the cakes in the untinted buttercream, spreading it evenly with a palette knife.

7 Sprinkle shredded (desiccated) coconut over the top of the cake. Tip the board a little to sprinkle it on the sides, until it is all covered.

Tip

You can be creative with your candy and use any that take your fancy. Frosty can even have four different types of buttons if you wish!

8 Use the leaf-shaped piece of cake you cut out, together with the cupcake to make the snowman's hat. Cut them to the shape you want, cover them in the red buttercream, and put them at the top of the snowman's head.

9 Give the snowman eyes, mouth, and buttons. If you use the same candies as we have, cut the licorice in half for the eyes and arrange the chocolate chips for the mouth. Position the sugar-coated candies down the center as buttons.

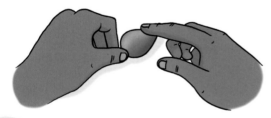

10 Tint the fondant icing orange using the food coloring paste and shape it into a carrot for Frosty's nose.

11 Finally, tie the ribbon around Frosty's neck and push a chocolate flake into each side for the arms.

Wise owl

This is a cake for chocolate lovers. It's easy to decorate using chocolate sprinkles, different sized chocolate buttons, and chocolate bars. You'll enjoy making them into this wise old owl. No eating the chocolates before you have finished!

You will need

2 quantities Medium Vanilla or Chocolate Cake (see page 21)

1 quantity Chocolate Fudge Frosting (see page 28)

chocolate buttons in different sizes

chocolate vermicelli

1 flaked chocolate bar

1 chocolate-covered toffee bar

2 x 9-in. (23-cm) round cake pans

non-stick baking parchment

piping bag, fitted with a star tip (nozzle)

serves 12–16

1 Ask an adult to help you preheat the oven to 350°F (180°C) Gas 4. Lightly grease each cake pan with a little soft butter and then line the base with a circle of baking parchment (see page 8).

2 Make the cake batter and divide it between the two prepared cake pans. Ask an adult to help you put them on the middle shelf of the preheated oven and bake for 30–35 minutes, or until a skewer inserted into the middle of the cakes comes out clean. Let the cakes cool in the pans for 10 minutes before turning out onto a wire rack. Turn the cakes right side up and let cool. While the cakes are cooling, make the Chocolate Fudge Frosting (see page 28).

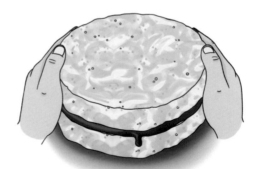

3 Cutting horizontally, use a long, serrated knife to level the tops of the cakes (see page 32). Place one cake on a serving plate and spread the cut surface with about 3 tablespoons of the Chocolate Fudge Frosting. Put the other cake on top, cut side down. Cover the top and sides of the whole cake with three-quarters of the remaining Chocolate Fudge Frosting, spreading evenly with a palette knife.

4 Arrange the chocolate buttons over the bottom half of the cake to look like feathers. Begin just below halfway down on the left and make a line of buttons around the bottom edge of the cake, with each button just overlapping the one next to it. Go back to the beginning and start again with this row overlapping the first. Keep going for about four rows, depending on the size of the chocolate buttons. Sprinkle the top half of the cake with chocolate vermicelli.

TOO-WHIT, too-whoo!

5 Fill the piping bag with the remaining Chocolate Fudge Frosting and use this to pipe feathers around the owl's face (see page 43 for more on piping). Start each feather about 1 in. (2.5 cm) from the edge and pipe to the edge at an angle.

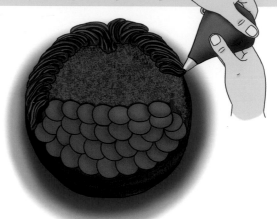

6 Build up different types of chocolate buttons to make eyes with a dab of frosting to stick them together.

7 Using a sharp knife, press down gently onto a board to cut the chocolate flake into thin pieces. Push them into the bottom edge of the cake to make legs. Cut the toffee bar in half. Slice one half diagonally into two pieces for the wings and push one into each side of the owl. Cut the remaining toffee bar to make a pointed beak.

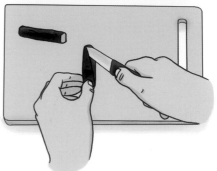

Teddy bear cake

This would be the perfect cake to make for a younger brother or sister's birthday. The cute smile is made out of delicious chocolate candy. You will have four cupcakes left over when you have made your bear, so you can check how good your cake is before the party!

You will need

1 quantity Large Vanilla or Chocolate Cake (see page 21)

1 quantity Small Vanilla or Chocolate Cake (see page 21)

1 quantity Chocolate Fudge Frosting (see page 28)

assorted chocolate drops and buttons

2 x 8-in. (20-cm) round cake pans

non-stick baking parchment

12-hole muffin pan, lined with 6 paper cupcake cases and 1 mini paper cupcake case

large plate or board with room for the cake and the ears

ribbon

serves 10

1 Preheat the oven. Ask an adult to help you turn the oven on to 350°F (180°C) Gas 4, so it will be hot by the time you are ready to bake.

2 Put one of the round cake pans on the baking parchment and draw around it twice to make two circles. Cut them out. Scoop a little soft butter onto a paper towel and rub this all over the inside of the pans. Put the parchment circles into the bases of the pans and leave to one side.

3 Make the LARGE quantity of cake batter and spoon it evenly into the two pans. Ask an adult to help you put it onto the middle shelf of the oven for about 30 minutes. Check that the cakes are done by pushing a metal skewer into the middle of one. If it comes out clean, the cake is cooked. Leave them to cool in the pan for about 10 minutes before turning out onto a wire rack. Turn them the right way up and leave to cool completely.

4 While the big cake is cooking, make the SMALL quantity of cake batter. Spoon the batter into the mini cake case first and then evenly into the other cake cases. Ask an adult to help you put these onto the middle shelf of the oven and set a timer for 15 minutes. When the timer goes off, take out the mini cake and set the timer for another 10 minutes to finish cooking the other cupcakes. Leave the cakes in the tin to cool for 10 minutes and then move them to the wire rack to cool completely.

5 Make the Chocolate Fudge Frosting (see page 28) while the cakes are cooling.

6 Use a long, serrated knife to level the tops of the big cakes, if they are not flat (see page 32). Place one cake on the serving plate and spread 3–4 tablespoons of chocolate frosting over the top. Put the second cake on top. Use three-quarters of the remaining chocolate frosting to cover the top and sides of the whole cake, spreading it evenly with a palette knife.

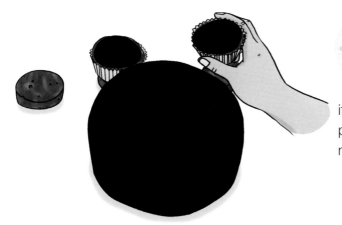

7 Cover the tops of two cupcakes with frosting. These are the teddy's ears but they will need to be raised, so peel the paper case off another cupcake and cut it in half horizontally. Put one half under each ear and put the ears in their place by the head. The ears should now be roughly the same height as the cake.

8 Peel the paper case off the mini cupcake and completely cover it with frosting. Put it in the middle of the cake to make the teddy's nose. Arrange the chocolate drops on the face for the eyes, mouth, and ears. Make a bow out of the ribbon and place at the teddy's neck.

TEA-TIME teddy!

Easter bunny cake

The chocolate bunny and the cute marzipan carrots on this very special carrot cake will make it into the star of your Easter feast. This is a longer project than some of the other cakes. You will need to make the carrots a day ahead, so that the color doesn't run into the frosting when you decorate it. You also need to prepare your ingredients (grate carrots!) before you begin mixing up the cake. This cake keeps well so you could make it one day, wrap it in plastic wrap, or put it in an airtight container and ice it the next day.

You will need

For the cake

½ cup (75 g) shelled pecans

2¾ cups (375 g) all-purpose (plain) flour

2 teaspoons baking powder

1 teaspoon baking soda (bicarbonate of soda)

½ teaspoon ground cinnamon

3 large (UK medium) eggs

1½ cups (375 ml) groundnut (peanut) or sunflower oil

2¼ cups (450 g) unrefined superfine (golden caster) sugar

4 tablespoons milk

1 teaspoon vanilla extract

1 lb. (500 g) carrots, grated

grated zest of 1 unwaxed orange

1 cup (125 g) shredded (desiccated) coconut

For the carrots

3½ oz. (100 g) marzipan

orange food coloring paste

angelica

For the frosting

1 lb. (450 g) cream cheese

2–3 heaping tablespoons honey

chocolate rabbit

2 x 8-in. (20-cm) round cake pans

non-stick baking parchment

serves 8–10

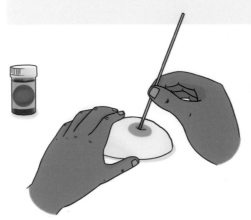

1 The day before you make the cake, tint the marzipan orange. Dip a toothpick or wooden skewer into the paste and then push it into the marzipan. Knead the marzipan until it is an even orange all over. If the color is too light add some more paste and knead again until it is a strong orange.

2 Put a piece of baking parchment into an airtight container. Break off a grape-sized piece of marzipan and roll it between your hands into a carrot shape. Keep making carrots until you have used up all the marzipan. Using the blunt end of a wooden skewer push a small hole into the top of each carrot. Put the carrots into the container, put the lid on, and let them dry overnight.

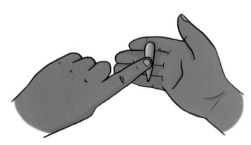

3 Now for the cake. Ask an adult to turn the oven on to 350°F (180°C) Gas 4, so it will be hot by the time you are ready to bake. Prepare the two cake pans. Put one of the round cake pans on the baking parchment and draw around it twice to make two circles. Cut them out. Scoop a little soft butter onto a paper towel and rub this all over the inside of the pans. Put the parchment circles into the bases of the pans and leave to one side.

4 Peel the carrots with a potato peeler, cut off the ends, and grate them. If an adult is helping, it is very quick to do this in a food processor. Otherwise, you will need to use a grater and it will take you quite a long time! Use the coarse side of the grater (with big holes). Be careful not to grate your fingers. Never try to grate very small pieces of carrot. Put the grated carrot into a bowl and leave to one side.

5 Now use the fine (small holes) side of the grater to grate the zest of the orange onto a plate. Only grate the colored surface of the peel. The white pith beneath is bitter and you don't want any in your mix. Keep turning the fruit to find ungrated peel. Put to one side.

6 Put the pecans on a baking sheet and ask an adult to help you put them in the hot oven. Roast them for about 7 minutes but watch them—they burn very easily and you may need to take them out sooner. Tip them onto a chopping board, then let them cool before cutting them roughly into smaller pieces, with an adult supervising you. Keep one hand on the handle and the other flat on top of the blade as you cut. Put to one side.

7 Sift the flour, baking powder, baking soda (bicarbonate of soda), and cinnamon together into a bowl and put to one side.

8 Carefully break the eggs into another bowl and fish out any pieces of shell. Whisk them to break up the yolks. Add the oil, sugar, milk, and vanilla extract and keep whisking until the mixture is smooth.

9 Add the grated carrots, orange zest, shredded (desiccated) coconut, and chopped pecans and use a wooden spoon to mix everything together.

10 Add half the flour to the mixture and fold it in. To fold, use a metal spoon to cut through the mixture in a gentle figure of eight. Don't beat or over-stir it—gentle folding traps air into the mixture and will make the cake lovely and light. When the flour is mixed in, add the second half and do the same.

11 Spoon the mixture into the two cake pans, making sure you put the same amount in each pan. Use a soft spatula to scrape out the bowl and then level the tops of the cakes.

12 Ask an adult to help you put the pans on the middle shelf of the oven. Set the timer for 40 minutes. To check if the cakes are cooked, push a metal skewer into the center of one. If it is clean when you take it out the cake is cooked. If it is covered with sticky mixture it needs a bit longer. Let the cakes cool in the pans for 10 minutes.

13 Run a blunt knife around the edge of the pan to loosen the cake. Place a plate on top of one cake pan and then turn the tray and pan upside down so that the cake drops out onto the plate. Carefully turn it over and lift it onto a wire tray. Do the same for the other cake. Leave them until they are completely cold before you begin decorating.

14 To make the frosting, beat the cream cheese and honey together until smooth. Place one of the cake layers on a large plate and spread half the frosting over it. Place the other cake on top and spread the other half of the frosting over this. It doesn't need to be smooth!

15 With the point of a sharp knife, cut the angelica into thin slices about 1 in. (2.5 cm) long. (This is fiddly so you may want to ask an adult to help you.) Push a few slices into the end of each carrot. Place your chocolate bunny on the cake and surround it with tasty carrots.

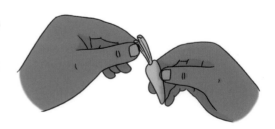

The EASTER bunny loves carrots!

Yule log

Bringing a special log into the house to burn in the fire in the middle of winter is a tradition that goes back thousands of years! Nowadays, we are more likely to have chocolate yule log like this one made from a sponge roll and decorated with Christmas decorations. Making a sponge roll is a fun new baking technique to try.

You will need

For the sponge cake

½ cup (115 g) superfine (caster) sugar

4 large (UK medium) eggs

½ teaspoon vanilla extract

1½ oz. (40 g) unsalted butter, plus extra for greasing the pan

generous 1 cup (135 g) all-purpose (plain) flour

½ teaspoon baking powder

For the filling and frosting

4–5 tablespoons chocolate hazelnut spread (Nutella)

3½ oz. (100 g) bittersweet (dark) chocolate

⅓ cup (100 ml) heavy (double) cream

confectioners' (icing) sugar, for sprinkling

your choice of decorations

8 x 12-in. (20 x 30-cm) jelly (Swiss) roll pan

non-stick baking parchment

serves 10

1 Ask an adult to turn the oven on to 400°F (200°C) Gas 6, so it will be hot by the time you are ready to bake. Put a little soft butter on a piece of kitchen paper and rub it around the inside of the pan to grease it. Cut two rectangles of baking parchment to fit the pan: set the pan on the paper, draw around it, then cut just inside the line. Fit one of them into the pan to completely cover the base.

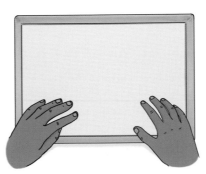

2 Put the sugar in a mixing bowl or the bowl of an electric mixer. Break the eggs into a small bowl, pick out any pieces of shell, then pour the eggs into the bowl with the sugar. Add the vanilla extract. Ask an adult to help you melt the butter in a small saucepan over a low heat, or in the microwave. Leave to cool until needed.

3 Using an electric whisk or the whisk attachment of the mixer, whisk the sugar and eggs together for 2 minutes, or until very thick and foamy. You could do this with a hand whisk but it's hard work and will take longer than 2 minutes!

Tip

Your cake ingredients should be at room temperature, so get everything out of the refrigerator a little while before you begin.

4 Set a strainer (sieve) over the bowl. Tip the flour and baking powder into the strainer and sift it into the bowl. Gently fold into the egg mixture with a large metal spoon. Do this slowly and carefully in a figure of eight pattern so the air isn't knocked out of the mixture. Drizzle the melted butter over the top and fold it in quite quickly.

5 Pour the mixture into the prepared pan and spread it evenly using a plastic scraper or spatula. Ask an adult to help you put the sponge in the oven to bake for 10 minutes. To test if the sponge is cooked ,press the center lightly with a finger; if the cake is springy it is cooked, if your finger leaves a dent cook for 2 more minutes then test again.

Safety Tip

Always remember to put on oven mitts before you put something into the oven, as well as when you take it out.

6 Ask an adult to help you remove the sponge from the oven. Leave for 1 minute to cool. Meanwhile place the second sheet of baking parchment on the work surface. Ask an adult to help you tip the sponge out onto the parchment. Carefully peel off the lining parchment. Then, using the edge of the tin as a ruler (being careful not to burn your hand) and a sharp knife, score a line right across one short side of the cake, about 1 in. (2.5 cm) from the edge, only cutting down half way. Be very careful not to cut right through the cake. This score line will help you when you begin to roll.

7 Starting at the cut end, gently lift the paper and sponge together and begin to roll up the sponge by folding over the scored line. Keep on rolling with the parchment still inside. Leave the sponge until it is completely cold.

8 Carefully unroll the sponge. Don't worry if the cake has cracked as all the cracks will be covered with frosting! Spread the chocolate spread over the sponge. Then use the parchment to help you lift the end of the cake and roll it again, but this time pull the paper away as you roll so that it doesn't end up inside! Put the cake on a serving plate while you make the frosting.

9 Break up the bittersweet (dark) chocolate and put it in a heatproof bowl. Put the cream in a small saucepan and ask an adult to help you heat the cream until it is steaming hot, but not boiling. Remove from the heat and then pour the hot cream into the bowl of chocolate pieces. Leave for 1 minute, then stir gently until smooth and melted. Leave until the mixture is thick enough to spread, about 1 hour.

10 Spread the cooled chocolate cream all over the top, ends, and sides of your cake. Run the prongs of a fork down the log so it looks like bark on a real tree. Put a little confectioners' (icing) sugar "snow" in a strainer (sieve) and shake it over the log. Add as many decorations as you like to the top of the log. Your Yule log is best stored in an airtight container in a cool place and eaten within 3 days.

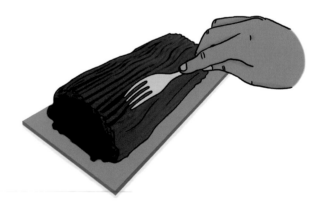

CHRISTMAS *is coming!*

Chocolate fudge birthday cake

This is a really delicious, chocolatey cake, perfect for birthdays—just decorate it and add candles! It tastes best when made the day before the party. You need four different bowls for this one, so make sure you wash up afterward!

You will need

For the cake

2¼ cups (250 g) all-purpose (plain) flour

2 teaspoons baking powder

1 teaspoon baking soda (bicarbonate of soda)

pinch of salt

3½ oz. (100 g) bittersweet (dark) chocolate

3 tablespoons cocoa powder

⅓ cup (100 ml) water, very hot but not boiling

1½ sticks (175 g) unsalted butter, softened

1½ cups (250 g) superfine (caster) sugar

3 large (UK medium) eggs

1 cup (200 ml) plain yogurt

For the decoration

⅓ cup (100 ml) heavy (double) cream

2 oz. (50 g) milk chocolate

2 oz. (50 g) bittersweet (dark) chocolate

selection of chocolate candies

9-in. (23-cm) springform cake pan

non-stick baking parchment

cake candles

serves 10–12

1 Ask an adult to help you preheat the oven to 350°F (180°C) Gas 4.

2 Grease the inside of the cake pan with a little soft butter on a piece of kitchen paper. Put the cake pan on the non-stick baking parchment and draw around it. Using scissors, cut inside the line so you have a circle the same size as the pan. Fit this into the bottom of the pan.

3 Set a large strainer (sieve) over a bowl and tip the flour, baking powder, baking soda (bicarbonate of soda), and salt into the strainer. Carefully sift these ingredients into the bowl. Put the bowl on one side until needed.

Tip
You can use any shop-bought decorations—or why not try making your own chocolate curls (see page 46)?

4 Break up the bittersweet (dark) chocolate and put it into a large heatproof mixing bowl. Add in the cocoa powder. Ask an adult to help you pour on the very hot water. Leave for 1 minute, then stir gently with a wooden spoon until the chocolate has all melted and the mixture is very smooth. Put to one side.

5 Put the butter and sugar into the bowl of an electric mixer or a mixing bowl. Beat well with the whisk attachment or a wooden spoon.

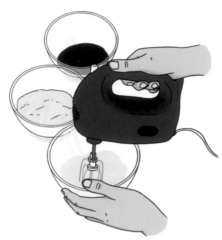

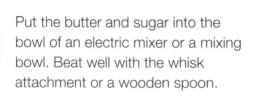

6 Break the eggs into a small bowl, remove any pieces of shell. Whisk with a fork until the mix is a bit frothy and the yolks have broken up, then gradually add the eggs to the sugar and butter and beat really well until very smooth.

7 Add the melted chocolate mixture to the bowl and mix well. Spoon in the yogurt, tip in the flour mixture, and mix well.

8 Spoon the mixture into the prepared pan, and smooth out the top with a spatula.

9 Ask an adult to help you put the cake in the oven to bake for 55 minutes. To test if it is cooked ask an adult to help you remove the cake from the oven and stick a skewer into the middle, then carefully pull it out—the cake is cooked if the skewer comes out clean. If the skewer is sticky, then bake for another 5 minutes and test again. Remove the cake from the oven and set the pan on a wire rack. Leave to cool for 5 minutes then loosen the cake by running a round-bladed knife inside the pan. Unclip the pan and leave the cake to cool completely. Don't worry if it sinks a bit.

10 To make the frosting, put the cream into a saucepan. Ask an adult to help you heat it until it is hot but not quite boiling. Remove the pan from the heat. Break up the two kinds of chocolate and put it into a heatproof bowl. Carefully pour over the hot cream. Leave for about 2 minutes then stir until smooth. Leave to cool. The frosting will thicken as it cools.

11 Set the cake upside down on a serving plate. Spread the icing on the top and sides of the cake to cover it completely (see page 38 for more help on this). Decorate with sprinkles, candies, and candles. Leave in a cool place until it is firm before you cut it. Store your cake in an airtight container and eat it within 5 days.

Don't forget the CANDLES!

Marmalade cat

If you are a cat lover, this is the cake for you. This is a ginger cat but you could make an all-white one with pink ears, a black and white one, a gray one, or even a tabby; choose your colors and make your own design.

You will need

1 quantity Medium Vanilla Cake (see page 21)

1 quantity Large Vanilla Cake (see page 21)

1 quantity Buttercream (see page 27)

orange food coloring paste

2 green fruit pastilles or other green candy

1 small licorice candy

1 long licorice shoelace

black writing icing

7-in. (18-cm) round cake pan

9-in. (23-cm) round cake pan

non-stick baking parchment

large serving board

serves 12–14

1 Preheat the oven. Ask an adult to help you turn the oven on to 350°F (180°C) Gas 4, so it will be hot by the time you are ready to bake.

2 Put the cake pans on the baking parchment and draw around them. Cut out the circles. Scoop a little soft butter onto a paper towel and rub this all over the inside of the pans. Put the parchment circles into the bases of the pans and leave to one side.

3 Make the LARGE quantity of cake batter and spoon it into the large pan. Ask an adult to help you put it onto the middle shelf of the oven for about 35–40 minutes. Check that the cake is done by pushing a metal skewer into the middle. If it comes out clean the cake is cooked. Leave it to cool in the pan for about 10 minutes before turning out onto a wire rack. Turn it the right way up and leave to cool completely.

The purr-fect cake for all!

4 While the big cake is cooking, make the MEDIUM quantity of cake batter. Spoon the batter into smaller pan. Follow step 3 again but cook this cake for 30 minutes. Remember it must be cold before you begin decorating.

5 Use a long, serrated knife to level the tops of the cakes and make them the same height (see page 32). This can be quite tricky so ask an adult to help. Take the smaller cake pan and hold it on top of the big cake where the cat's head will be (overlapping the big cake by about 3 in./8 cm). Use a skewer to draw around the pan, scratching the surface of the cake.

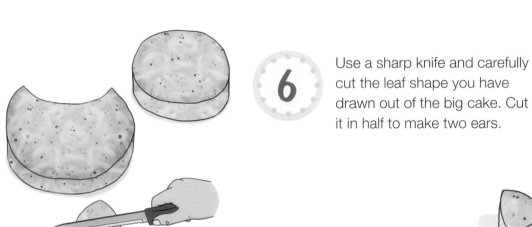

6 Use a sharp knife and carefully cut the leaf shape you have drawn out of the big cake. Cut it in half to make two ears.

7 Place the large cake on the serving board and fit the smaller cake into the space you have cut out. Position the ears at the top of the smaller cake.

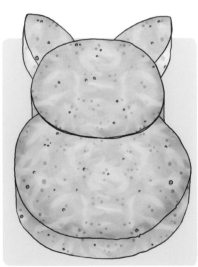

8 Make the buttercream frosting. Take out 4–5 tablespoons and put it in a small bowl and leave to one side. Tint the remaining buttercream orange with orange food coloring paste.

9 Cover the cat with the orange buttercream, spreading it evenly with a palette knife. Carefully spread the untinted buttercream on top to make a tummy shape and use a small rounded knife to spread it inside the ears.

Tip

Don't worry about trying to spread the buttercream too neatly— it's supposed to look like fur!

10 Design the cat's face. Use the green fruit pastilles for the eyes. Slice the licorice candy into thin slices to make the nose. Use the licorice shoelace to make the tail and the mouth. Use the black writing icing to draw on the whiskers and the pupils in the eyes.

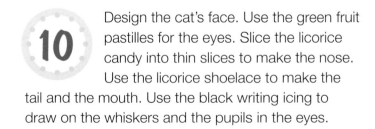

Snakes and ladders

This big cake will challenge your icing skills and will need you to use a ruler and some math, but it's definitely worth it for a stunning result. Maybe you should find some dice and play a game on it before you eat it. Use colored sweets as counters and the winner can have the first slice!

You will need

2 quantities Medium Vanilla Cake (see page 21)

1 quantity Buttercream (see page 27)

2 lb. (1 kg) white ready-to-roll fondant icing

green food coloring paste

yellow food coloring paste

black writing icing

assorted gummy snakes

10-in. (25-cm) square cake pan

non-stick baking parchment

ribbon (optional)

serves 15–20

1 Ask an adult to help you turn the oven on to 350°F (180°C) Gas 4 so it will be hot by the time you are ready to bake. Draw around the cake pan on baking parchment and cut out the square piece. Put it in the base of the pan and use some butter on a piece of paper towel to grease all over the parchment and the sides of the pan.

2 Make the Vanilla Cake batter (see page 21), but remember that you are using double quantities of all the ingredients, so make sure you use a really big mixing bowl. Spoon the batter into the cake pan.

3 Ask an adult to help you put the cake on the middle shelf of the preheated oven and bake for 40–45 minutes, or until a skewer inserted into the middle of the cake comes out clean. Let the cake cool in the pan for 10 minutes before carefully loosening it all around the edge with a palette knife and turning it out onto a wire rack. Turn the cake right side up and let cool completely. While it is cooling make up the quantity of buttercream (see page 27).

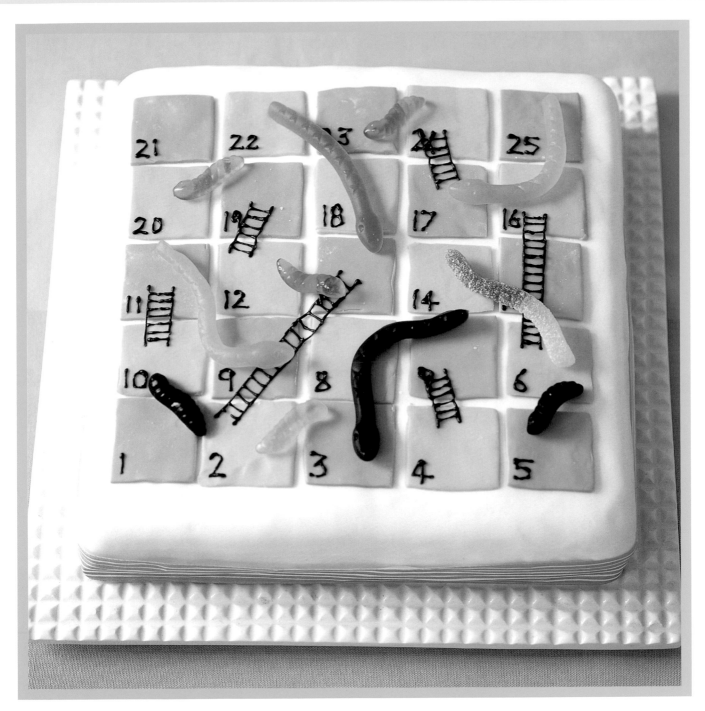

Roll the dice and PLAY!

4 When it is cold put the cake on a board. You may need to cut a thin layer off the top so it is flat. Cut horizontally with a long, serrated bread knife to do this (see page 32).

5 Carefully spread buttercream over the whole cake using a palette knife to make it smooth and even.

6 Now measure the height of your cake. If it is 3 in. (8 cm) high, you will need a square of fondant icing with sides that are 16 in. (10 in. + 3 in. + 3 in./25 cm + 8 cm + 8 cm = 41 cm).

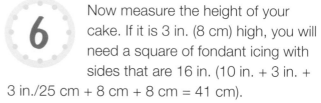

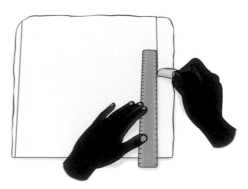

7 Cut off one quarter of the fondant icing and wrap it in plastic wrap (clingfilm) to use later. Lightly dust your work surface with confectioners' (icing) sugar. Roll out the rest of the fondant icing so that it is big enough to cut out a square with sides the length you have just worked out. This is a big piece of icing to roll. Keep lifting the edges to check it isn't sticking and add more sugar if it is. Try to get it an even thickness.

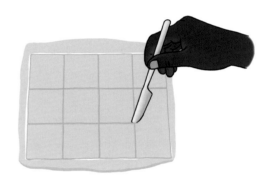

8 You may need some help with this step. Place the buttercream-covered cake near to you and dust your hands with confectioners' (icing) sugar. Carefully lift the fondant icing by sliding both hands under it, taking care not to tear any holes in it. Position it over the cake and then smooth over the top—this will get rid of any trapped air bubbles. Pinch the icing together at the corners and then cut off the triangle of excess icing. Cut off any excess around the base (see pages 39–40) for more on covering cakes with fondant).

9 Cut the remaining icing in half. Keep one half wrapped in plastic wrap (clingfilm) and tint the other yellow (see page 36). Sprinkle your work surface with confectioners' (icing) sugar and roll out the yellow icing until you have a rectangle of icing that is 6½ x 5 in. (16 x 12 cm). Mark off every 1½ in. (4 cm) along each side and join the dots to make 12 squares, each with sides of 1½ in. (4 cm). Cut them out along the lines. Now tint the other half of the icing green and roll this out to a long rectangle that is 11 x 3 in. (28 x 8 cm). Divide it up into 1½-in. (4-cm) squares as before but cut one extra, as you need 13 green squares.

10 Arrange the squares in a checkerboard pattern with the green squares in each of the corners. Then lift each square in turn, brush a little cooled boiled water on the bottom, and stick it back down on the cake. Let the icing dry overnight in an airtight container.

11 The next day, use the writing icing to draw numbers and ladders on the squares and arrange the gummy snakes. If you have a ribbon, tie it around the bottom of the cake.

Prickly hedgehog

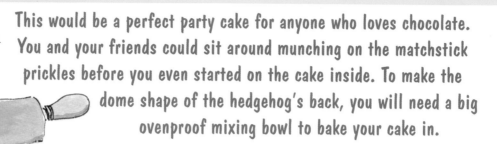

This would be a perfect party cake for anyone who loves chocolate. You and your friends could sit around munching on the matchstick prickles before you even started on the cake inside. To make the dome shape of the hedgehog's back, you will need a big ovenproof mixing bowl to bake your cake in.

You will need

....

soft butter, for greasing

flour, for dusting

1 quantity Large Vanilla or Chocolate Cake (see page 21)

1 quantity Small Vanilla or Chocolate Cake (see page 21)

1 quantity Chocolate Fudge Frosting (see page 28)

chocolate vermicelli

about 1 lb. (500 g) chocolate mint matchsticks (3–4 boxes)

3 chocolate drops

2-quart (2-liter) ovenproof glass bowl,

6-hole muffin pan, lined with paper cases

large serving plate or board

serves 10

1 Preheat the oven. Ask an adult to turn the oven on to 350°F (180°C) Gas 4 so it will be hot by the time you are ready to bake.

2 Scoop some soft butter onto a paper towel and rub this all over the inside of the ovenproof glass bowl. Use quite a lot of butter because you can't use baking parchment to stop the cake sticking to the bowl. Now sprinkle one or two tablespoons of flour inside the bowl and keep tapping the sides and tipping the bowl until the whole surface is covered with flour, which sticks to the butter (this is called dusting). Tip out any loose flour.

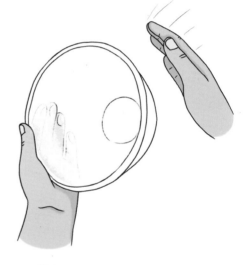

Tip

You only need to use one cupcake out of the six you make, but the rest can be frozen for another time.

3 Make the LARGE quantity of cake batter and spoon it into the prepared bowl. Level the top with a spatula. Ask an adult to help you put it onto the middle shelf of the oven for about 1 hour. Check that the cake is done by pushing a metal skewer into the middle. If it comes out clean the cake is cooked. Leave to cool in the bowl for about 10 minutes before turning it out onto a wire rack. Leave it to cool completely.

A spiny SPECTACULAR!

4 While the large cake is cooking make the SMALL quantity of cake batter. Spoon the batter into the cake cases so each has the same amount. Ask an adult to help you put these onto the middle shelf of the oven next to the big cake, and cook for 25 minutes. Write down what time the cakes should come out so you don't get muddled with the big cake! Leave the cake cases in the pan for 10 minutes and then move them to the wire rack to cool completely.

5 While the cake is cooling, make your chocolate fudge frosting (see page 28).

6 Ask an adult to help you with this next step as it is quite tricky (or see page 32). If the flat base of the cake is a bit uneven, use a long, serrated knife to cut it so it is flat. Then cut the cake into three even horizontal layers. Take the top layers off.

7 Place the bottom layer on the serving board and then put the cake back together, spreading about 3 tablespoons of frosting between each layer.

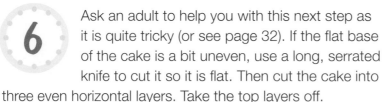

8 Cover the whole cake with the remaining chocolate frosting, spreading it evenly with a palette knife.

9 Peel the paper case off one cupcake and cut off the top so it is flat. Turn it upside down and cover it with frosting. Sprinkle the chocolate vermicelli over the top. Lift it carefully, using a palette knife underneath, and place it on the plate next to the big cake to make a head.

10 To make the spines, break the matchsticks in half. Push each half into the body of the hedgehog until it is totally covered in spines. Push the chocolate drops into the head for eyes and a nose.

Tip

Why not use your leftover cupcakes to make some cute baby hedgehogs? You can have a whole hedgehog family!

Templates

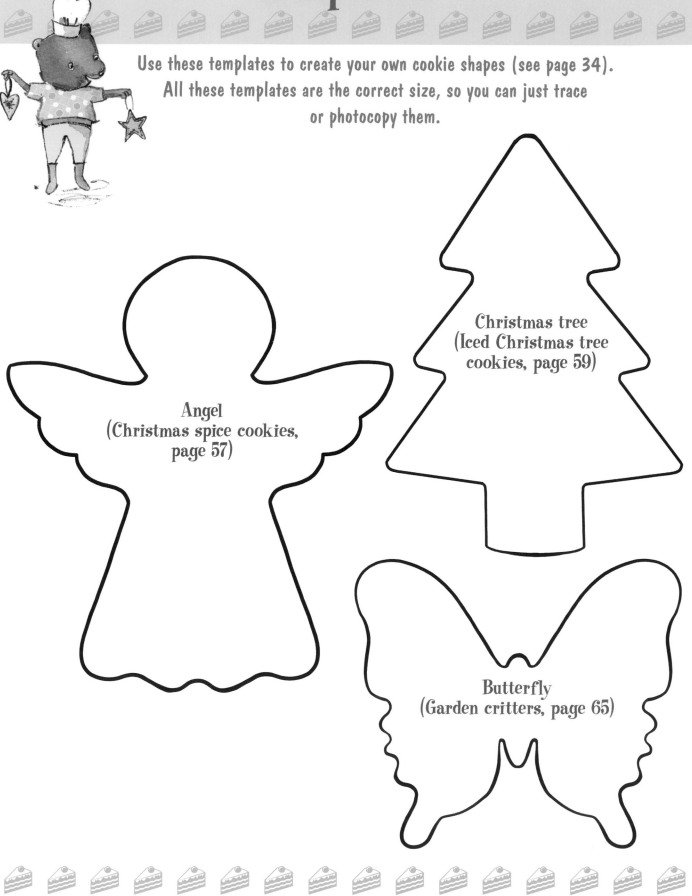

Use these templates to create your own cookie shapes (see page 34). All these templates are the correct size, so you can just trace or photocopy them.

Christmas tree
(Iced Christmas tree cookies, page 59)

Angel
(Christmas spice cookies, page 57)

Butterfly
(Garden critters, page 65)

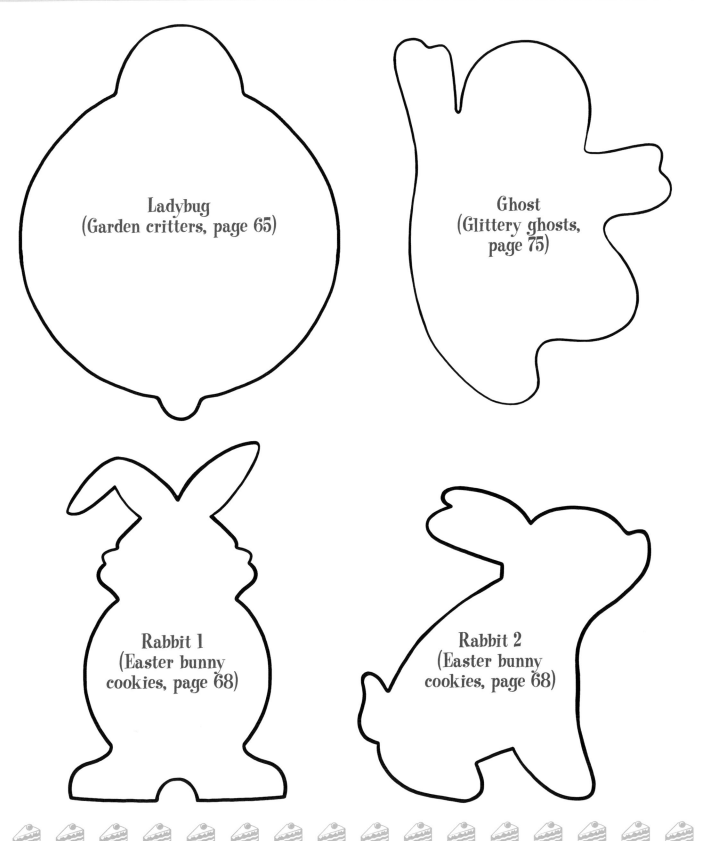

Ladybug
(Garden critters, page 65)

Ghost
(Glittery ghosts,
page 75)

Rabbit 1
(Easter bunny
cookies, page 68)

Rabbit 2
(Easter bunny
cookies, page 68)

Suppliers

Most of the projects in this book use ingredients and materials that you will already have in the kitchen or can buy at the supermarket, but for more specialist cake-decorating ingredients, you can try the following suppliers.

US Suppliers

Cake Art
www.cakeart.com

Fancy Flours Inc
www.fancyflours.com

Global Sugar Art
www.globalsugarart.com

Kitchen Krafts
www.kitchenkrafts.com

Michaels
www.michaels.com

The Baker's Cupboard
www.thebakerscupboard.com

Wilton
www.wilton.com

UK Suppliers

Cakes, Cookies & Crafts
www.cakescookiesandcrafts shop.co.uk

Hobbycraft
www.hobbycraft.co.uk

John Lewis
www.johnlewis.com

Lakeland
www.lakeland.co.uk

Make a Wish Cake Shop
www.makeawishcakeshop.co.uk

Squires Kitchen
www.squires-shop.com

Sugarshack
www.sugarshack.co.uk

Index

Credits

Recipes
Annie Rigg: pp.14, 17, 21, 27, 28, 29, 50, 59, 65, 72, 78, 82 86, 88, 92, 95, 98, 112, 116, 120
Linda Collister: pp. 57, 62, 103, 108
Chloe Coker 75

Photography
Brigdale, Martin p.46
Cassidy, Peter pp.15, 30
Davies, Vanessa pp.18, 62
Gregson, Jonathan p.45
Lane, Sandra pp.1, 30bl, 84, 85bl, 86, 93, 95, 99, 102, 113, 117, 118, 121
Linder, Lisa pp.3tr, 12, 16, 35, 51, 59, 61, 85tr, 89
West, Stuart pp.2, 3bl, 13bl, 23, 26, 69, 71, 75, 77
Whitaker, Kate pp.4, 6, 7, 13tr, 30tr, 37, 41, 42, 49, 52, 53br, 55, 65, 67, 73, 79, 83
Wreford, Polly pp.20, 53tl, 57, 103,107, 109